Enterprise Services Architecture

Dan Woods

Beijing · Cambridge · Farnham · Köln · Paris · Sebastopol · Taipei · Tokyo

Enterprise Services Architecture
by Dan Woods

Editor:	Dale Dougherty
Production Editor:	Darren Kelly
Cover Designer:	Edie Freedman
Interior Designer:	David Futato and Edie Freedman

Printing History:

September 2003:   First Edition.

 This book uses RepKover™, a durable and flexible lay-flat binding.

ISBN: 0-596-00551-2
[C]   [3/04]

Contents

Introduction

Perhaps the best way to look at the history of SAP is as a 30-year struggle with complexity. In the early days, we mostly sold through seminars. A group of CFOs or controllers would assemble to discuss how an accounting application should work. I or one of my cofounders would lead the discussion about the current version of our software and the audience would weigh in with a ferocious round of criticism and brainstorming. The CFOs would each offer their best ideas about how the accounting application should work and the leader of the seminar would moderate. It was like being back in grad school, except we were actually going to turn most of those ideas into a robust working system.

Of course, it took no time at all for the idea list to grow into the thousands. The essence of SAP's success in its first 10 years was the way that we selected from this list and created new versions of our products that were well-architected and flexible enough to become the foundation for the next round of improvements.

The principles behind this orderly expansion of our products is the essence of Enterprise Services Architecture, which is part engineering discipline and part computer science, applied to practical business problems.

Now pretty much every company is in the situation that SAP faced in its early years: they have an existing architecture and a long list of ideas, and they need to move quickly from version to version to keep up with their changing businesses.

The world is more complex now. We have web services, loosely coupled components, and all sorts of integration tools. We live in a heterogeneous world where many vendors' products are installed at a particular company. We realize it is a pipe dream to expect our customers to buy everyth solution they need from SAP. For that reason, SAP and other vendors will differentiate themselves going forward by helping companies manage the complexity of their system landscapes and build a coherent architecture in a heterogeneous world.

SAP's offer to help is contained in the vision of Enterprise Services Architecture explained in this book and in our SAP NetWeaver™ and SAP® xApps™ families of products. The Enterprise Services Architecture we describe is an application of service-oriented architecture and sound principles of object-oriented design applied to the current heterogeneous world of IT architecture. Enterprise services are the high-level components that aggregate web services into reusable elements with business value. Enterprise Services Architecture is an end-state in which the flexibility of the IT architecture matches the current and future needs of the enterprise, reduces the cost of change, and extends automation to new frontiers.

The new world of Enterprise Services Architecture will change the way all vendors build applications and the way companies use them. Monolithic applications will be broken apart into layers and offered as components. (For example, in the most recent version of mySAP™ Customer Relationship Management, the user interface was completely abstracted from the underlying application.) The reduced cost of integration and flexibility will make design, modeling, and architecture vital commodities as companies craft the optimal structure out of these components. The benefit should be the ability to optimize the business without a bottleneck in the IT infrastructure, which is too often the case.

This book is a tour of Enterprise Services Architecture from top to bottom. We invited the author, Dan Woods, inside the corporate mind of SAP to interview everyone involved in the project and report what he found. This is our second such collaboration, the first being the book on Packaged Composite Applications that was published earlier this year.

The ultimate goal of this book is to help our customers and the marketplace at large come to grips with the architectural revolution that is underway. After reading this volume, our sincere hope is that you feel better prepared to meet the challenges facing your company.

—Hasso Plattner
July 2003

Preface

This book is a top-to-bottom analysis of Enterprise Services Architecture, a concept that starts with service-oriented architecture and creates a useful road map from it based on sound computer science focused by economic reality. In a world of hype about web services and business process modeling, the program of architectural design and implementation described in Enterprise Services Architecture sounds a clear note about how to create business value.

This story and structure of Enterprise Services Architecture was extracted by mining the brain trust of SAP for all of the relevant arguments, examples, concepts, and analogies. As an author, I was allowed access to every corner of the engineering mother ship in Walldorf, Germany. I became a familiar figure in the cafeteria of SAP Labs in Palo Alto. I even got to learn the intricacies of software branding at Global Marketing Headquarters in New York City. What I found was an amazing consistency of thought. The story I tell in this book reflects a common understanding of where SAP has to go and how it will get there.

The book also benefited substantially from interviews with leading analysts like Josh Greenbaum of Enterprise Applications Consulting, Ravi Kalakota of E-Business Strategies, Yefim Natis and David Smith of Gartner Research, and Dan Sholler from MetaGroup. Adolf S. Allesch from Cap Gemini Ernst & Young weighed in with the systems integrator's perspective. Vinod Khosla generously agreed to speak from the venture capital point of view. John Hagel did not speak to me, but his book did, and for that I am thankful. Erik Gross, Eric

Soll, and Padman Ramankutty provided excellent examples of Enterprise Services Architecture in action. Andy Mulholland, CTO of Cap Gemini Ernst & Young, weighed in with a wonderful Afterword that greatly enhanced the book. I am especially grateful to Geoffrey Moore, a consultant, a venture capitalist, and a true gentleman who found time for the interview that became the basis for Chapter 9.

Chapter Summaries

This book explains Enterprise Services Architecture in nine chapters:

Chapter 1, *Concepts and Philosophy*
A tour through the ideas, the forces in the marketplace, technology developments, and the implications related to Enterprise Services Architecture.

Chapter 2, *In Practice*
Examples of how Enterprise Services Architecture builds on existing infrastructure and creates additional business value.

Chapter 3, *Making the Business Case*
Arguments for and against the adoption of Enterprise Services Architecture and the implementation of a service-oriented architecture based on components.

Chapter 4, *Anatomy*
A detailed analysis of the way that the Enterprise Services Architecture compliance levels interact with different parts of the existing IT infrastructure such as enterprise applications, open standards, platform component systems, and concepts from computer science.

Chapter 5, *The Platform*
A description of the software platform that enables the construction of components.

Chapter 6, *Applying Enterprise Services Architecture*
A description of a playbook and an analysis of the key questions that are involved in determining the right level of Enterprise Services Architecture compliance and the granularity of components in a company's IT architecture.

Chapter 7, *Creating a Road Map*
An analysis of the forces that come into play during an incremental implementation of Enterprise Services Architecture along with suggestions for successfully addressing difficult problems that retard progress.

Chapter 8, *The Enterprise Value Chain*
An analysis of how Enterprise Services Architecture will affect vendors of enterprise applications, technology platforms, and system integration services. The chapter also describes that architecture's impact on the internal workings of a company and relationships with partners and customers throughout the enterprise value chain.

Chapter 9, *Enterprise Services Architecture and Society*
An interview with Geoffrey Moore about the way Enterprise Services Architecture is changing vendors and companies and the impact that will have on the economy and society.

Afterword: *Enterprise Services Architecture and the Adaptive Enterprise*
Andy Mulholland, CTO of Cap Gemini Ernst & Young, describes how Enterprise Services Architecture relates to the concept of the Adaptive Enterprise.

Acronyms Used in This Book

For your reference, here is a list of the acronyms used in this book:

B2B	Business-to-Business
BPEL4WS	Business Process Execution Language for Web Services
BPML	Business Process Modeling Language
CRM	Customer Relationship Management
EAI	Enterprise Application Integration
ERP	Enterprise Resource Planning
ESA	Enterprise Services Architecture
HR	Human Resources
ISV	Independent software vendor

OASIS	Organization for the Advancement of Structured Information Standards
PCA	Packaged Composite Application
PLM	Product Lifecycle Management
ROI	Return on investment
SCM	Supply Chain Management
TCO	Total cost of ownership

How to Contact Us

We present strong arguments in favor of Enterprise Services Architecture in this book, but you may want to join in the debate. We welcome your voice. You can contact us at:

O'Reilly & Associates, Inc.
1005 Gravenstein Highway North
Sebastopol, CA 95472
(800) 998-9938 (in the United States or Canada)
(707) 829-0515 (international/local)
(707) 829-0104 (fax)

To ask technical questions or comment on the book, send email to:

bookquestions@oreilly.com

We have a web site for the book, where we'll list errata and any plans for future editions. You can access this page at:

http://www.oreilly.com/catalog/entservapps

For more information about this book and others, see the O'Reilly web site:

http://www.oreilly.com

Acknowledgments

This book is dedicated to the men and women of SAP, who spoke with one voice about Enterprise Services Architecture and made the process of writing this book the equivalent of an ongoing seminar on extracting business value from information technology. First, I would like to thank Hasso Plattner for thinking up the idea in the first place. Shai Agassi, Peter Graf, and Ori Inbar, the devoted sponsors of this project, helped it along at each stage with comments, encouragement, and suggestions on how to find the right information in the vast brain trust of SAP. Peter Zencke, Pascal Brosset, Mark Sochan, Rainer Brendle, Werner Aigner, Ruediger Buck Emden, Thomas Anton, Tim Bussiek, Peter Kuerpick, Juergen Kreutziger, Dennis Moore, Franz Josef Fritz, Jochen Puzicha, Klaus Krepplin, Peter Kirschbauer, Jim Hagemann Snabe, Archim Heimann, Nils Herzberg, Martin Kuehn, Michael Fichtner, Willi Zwerger, Stephan Schindewolf, Juergen Hagedorn, Henrik Stotz, Daniel Grassman, Gilad Parann-Nissany, Stefan Sigg, Martin Huvar, Timm Falter, Holger Meinert, Sven Leukert, Sven Guenther, Sunil Gupta, Guido Schroeder, and Kaj Van de Loo all went beyond the call of duty. They diverted themselves from jammed schedules, understood the mission of the book, and kept it on course with detailed points of view. I want to express an extra measure of gratitude to Jeffrey Word, whose creative mind spawned the idea of writing books about the ideas behind SAP's technology and who realized that O'Reilly was the right publisher. Jason Wolf's team, especially Jennifer Huntington and Scott Feldman, provided unique access to SAP customers. Ajit Nazre deftly described the eBay integration. Sami Muneer was once again the most thorough and prolific reviewer, and I renew my call for his emergence as a writer. Conrad Voorsanger was generously roped into reviewing the first chapter and provided some excellent insight that improved the entire manuscript. Matthias Haendly and Thomas Mattern were the gardeners of this book. They created the necessary conditions that allowed the project to succeed. In addition to their full-time jobs, they arranged an endless parade of meetings and interviews. I would also like to thank Dale Dougherty and Mark Jacobson of O'Reilly for bringing me into this project, and Deb Cameron, whose advice and coaching were once again invaluable.

—Dan Woods

1

Concepts and Philosophy

The headlines in Silicon Valley in the summer of 2003 are about mergers instead of the latest new thing. Larger companies are grasping for smaller ones. Sectors are consolidating. Pundits are declaring that the entire Information Technology (IT) industry is a commodity, a tool for cost-cutting rather than innovation.

This tornado of hype explaining how companies should react to improve their competitive position offers little of practical value. What is impossible to reduce to a headline, sound bite, or glib analysis are the choices companies should make for their own IT architectures.

At the core of the forces generating the latest news is the widespread recognition that the land-grab phase of the IT industry is over. The industry is growing up. One can look at the growth of IT as the gradual extension of automation, starting with financial applications on the mainframe and then extending out through the personal computer, workstations, client/server, and the Internet as well as through applications for Enterprise Resources Planning, Human Resources, Customer Relationship Management, Supply Chain Management, and so on.

For almost every need there is a product, but each is a world unto itself. They don't talk to each other well or share data easily. Valuable services trapped inside are not reusable.

At the same time, companies are becoming aware that IT should help by automating and optimizing the processes of a business. But understanding of processes has evolved beyond the capability of

1

existing enterprise applications. Processes cross the boundaries of enterprise applications and extend beyond the boundaries of the company itself to suppliers, distributors, and customers. Automating processes across these boundaries is difficult and expensive. IT has become a bottleneck retarding the next phase of automation.

Portal technology that brings together functions from a variety of applications can help. The emergence of web services, XML-based standards, and other integration technology will make improving the situation easier. But for the next five years and beyond, it is clear that just slapping portals and web services onto existing enterprise applications will not solve the problem of unbounded process automation. The underlying applications are not ready to play that game.

Enterprise Services Architecture describes the solution. It is the blueprint, the set of principles, the values used to form a coherent answer to all of the questions facing companies today. The concept was hatched in 2002 in the mind of Hasso Plattner, the chairman of SAP AG, as he struggled to conceive of the next mountain his customers would have to climb. The concept, which builds on the principles applied during 30 years of company history, has bubbled through SAP and resulted in the creation of SAP xApps and SAP NetWeaver, technologies that enable a company to make progress toward an architecture that embodies Enterprise Services Architecture principles. But Enterprise Services Architecture is not an SAP product or even a product at all. Instead, it is a philosophy that guides the evolution of IT architecture along a path toward increased business value.

The core of Enterprise Services Architecture is a layer of components that coalesces data and application functionality from enterprise applications into useful and reusable modules. The components communicate using enterprise services. These services reduce the complexity of the connections among components to allow for reuse. The transition is similar to imagining a plate of spaghetti and meatballs transforming into a set of tinker toys. The meatballs (the components) become more structured and the spaghetti (the nest of complex connections) disappears, replaced by more clearly defined and structured relationships expressed as services.

Architecture is essentially a set of decisions and choices that one will have to live with for a long time. Enterprise Services Architecture is an analysis and a program for making those choices, based on the state of the IT industry and basic economics, to optimize the business value that is produced from investment in technology.

This book will explain what Enterprise Services Architecture is for the senior management and IT professionals who stand at the threshold of tremendous opportunity and who are, at the same time, being pursued by increasing threats on all sides.

The right architecture for any given company is a matter of crafting the best possible response to its competitive position. In IT strategy the landscape consists of multiple departments or divisions of the company, each with multiple suppliers, all working to create products and services for an increasingly competitive market.

In his book *Management Challenges for the 21st Century* (Harper-Business), Peter Drucker points out that one of the fallacies of management theory over the past 80 years has been the assumption of one right organization for a corporation. This notion applies to IT architecture as well. Enterprise Services Architecture is not a description of a single correct architecture but rather a description of important questions to ask about IT systems and a pattern for successful individualized answers that take into account the existing infrastructure and business conditions of our time.

If this book succeeds in its mission, it will help executives discover what Enterprise Services Architecture means to them, and most importantly what to do about it.

In the following pages, we will take a trip through all of the issues surrounding Enterprise Services architecture including:

- The business drivers putting pressure on companies to be more flexible
- The technology that enables the construction of components and services

- The structure of the Enterprise Services Architecture platform that brings Enterprise Services to life to create business value
- The challenges implicit in designing and implementing Enterprise Services Architecture at a company
- The effect that Enterprise Services Architecture will have on companies, technology vendors, and our economy at large

The IT industry is not the first to grow up in this manner. We will now take a look at the automobile industry, which followed a path of increased abstraction and componentization in the pursuit of efficiency and flexibility.

Components in Lean Manufacturing

Automobiles used to be thought of as large collections of parts. Each model was a world unto itself, a monolith, assembled from thousands of unique parts. Few parts were shared across cars or car makers. This structure amplified complexity and dramatically increased design, manufacturing, and maintenance costs. In the past 20 years, car makers have replaced the notion of thousands of parts with the idea of a much smaller number of subsystems. These subsystems fit together in standardized ways and are assembled in a particular order. The brakes, the transmission, the engine, and the steering mechanism all have the equivalent of plugs and sockets on them.

This approach has been adopted in every other sort of manufacturing, from watches to cell phones to vacuum cleaners. Componentization has not reduced complexity—cars are more complex than ever—but it has made manufacturing more manageable and less costly. At first, the components were used within the models of one car maker, but now they have spread so different firms use the same standardized components. This approach is called *lean manufacturing*.*

---

* For details of this transformation, see *The Machine That Changed The World: The Story of Lean Production* by James Womack, Daniel T. Jones, and Daniel Roos (HarperCollins).

This transformation did not occur overnight, and some firms proved better at it than others. In general, Japanese firms still lead American companies in adopting this approach. They use components extensively and design the car up front. Design is the province of the car maker while implementation details are handled by suppliers.

Enterprise Services Architecture is lean manufacturing for IT. It represents the imperative to componentize according to a standard architecture. Business software is actually much more complex than an automobile. With its myriad data elements, interfaces, and algorithms, a fully functional ERP system is many times more complex than a car. Because software is so pliable, we sometimes think that developing software must be easier than making physical objects. The truth is that the complexity is mind-boggling and should be approached with humility.

Enterprise Services Architecture offers companies a coherent plan for playing the role of car maker. The equivalent of the thousands of parts of the old-style manufacturing mode is the siloed complexity of applications. The equivalent of the standardized components of lean manufacturing is the sort of components that are created in an Enterprise Services Architecture platform. To make this transition a company must understand its processes and its current enterprise applications and then determine where it needs to build components that allow for the flexibility that business conditions increasingly demand.

The IT industry is very early in this cycle. Components exist only at the level of core technology. Relational databases are the best example, while web servers and browsers are the most recent. But even these components are fuzzy compared with components in manufacturing. Relational databases, for example, are standardized only to a degree. Products from different vendors have significant differences in core areas such as how to write procedures that are executed in response to various database events.

IT infrastructure is like aircraft. When a plane gets upgraded, most of its structure stays in place and continues to do its job. Companies over the past 30 years have built a tremendously complex infrastructure that has gone through several cycles from mainframe, to client/server, to Internet applications, and now to composite applications, which build on the existing infrastructure.

Technology succeeds and stays in place in the long-term because it addresses a business problem. Legacy systems are systems that work. One of the core values of Enterprise Services Architecture is accepting this fact and keeping existing systems in place, encapsulating them in abstractions at the right level, componentizing them when necessary, and then building new systems using them as parts.

Standards Are Vital

A major implication of these trends is a dramatic rise in the importance of standards. The proliferation of interfaces between companies and between components in companies gives standardization a value it did not have in the past. A tiered architecture relies on standard ways of communicating. In the early stages, the entity with the most power dictates to less powerful partners how they will do business. Wal-Mart did not wait around for a standards body to approve its vendor-managed interfaces. It explained politely to its partners that supporting the interfaces was a requirement of doing business with Wal-Mart. It is now doing the same thing with radio frequency identification (RFID) technology, which is used to automatically identify products via electronic scanning. From the standpoint of mergers and acquisitions, divisions that adhere to standards may fetch a higher price because they offer smooth integration with a new owner.

Standardization can result in increased customer adoption, better customer service, and improved product quality. The GSM wireless standard adopted across Europe enables every wireless vendor to compete in every other country, and the resulting competition has created much more advanced wireless services than in the United States.

Supporting emerging industry standards and participating in their design can be another source of competitive advantage. Enterprise Services Architecture with its emphasis on abstraction and componentization is a perfect mechanism for adapting to and implementing the increasing number of internal and external standards required for doing business.

Standardization took place in the manufacturing industry over the past several decades. In automobile manufacturing, at first only smaller parts like spark plugs and batteries became standard components. Within a manufacturer, chassis, transmissions, and brake assemblies became common across models. Third parties started manufacturing components that were used by multiple manufacturers.

The key to componentization on a mass scale is standardization. Third parties could not make components that would be used across manufacturers without some sort of standard for what the component would do and how it would fit into other components. Over time these standards evolve. Aircraft get updated over their 25-year lifetime with different engines and other subsystems.

Standards have two parts: the design of the individual components and the design of the architecture as a whole that make sense of how all of the components fit together. The challenge of Enterprise Services Architecture is to create an environment for IT where standardized components can work together without a return to monolithic complexity. To create really reusable components, we need an infrastructure that allows components to adapt to the needs of the environment. We also need an environment that is able to adapt to plugged-in components.

Even in manufacturing, standards followed; they did not lead. To gain the benefits of flexibility, lower costs, and the ability to customize to meet market demands, manufacturers componentized their products prior to adoption of standards across the industry. Those in the IT industry who wait for standards to improve their architecture will be waiting quite a while and will lose out on the business benefits of Enterprise Services Architecture in the meantime.

The Business Drivers for Flexibility

The fragmented world of data and software would really not be much of a problem if business conditions remained constant, as they did in the early 1990s before the arrival of the Internet as a primary force. Back then, most companies were self-contained units, impenetrable to the outside, and IT systems were an internal affair. A painful and clunky user interface was not a large problem. The people using the software were employees, usually with highly specialized functions, and they would make do because they had to.

Now the network has brought suppliers and customers right inside that infrastructure. Customers frequently use computer interfaces to a company's systems, often through the Internet. This computer-mediated interaction with customers applies not just in a few industries and contexts, like customers interacting with a bank through an ATM or with an airline reservations system through a web site, but it has spread to almost every company. Customers become angry if an interface is awkward or if the system is slow. They are insulted if they show up at one touchpoint of the company and it becomes clear that the underlying application is trapped in a silo and does not does not know about the other relationships with the company that are trapped in other silos.

At the business-to-business level, creating the most efficient supply chain involves opening up the core systems of the company and integrating them with vendors' systems at key points. Under the vendor-managed inventory paradigm that Wal-Mart has made famous, orders automatically flow from stores to suppliers based on how fast products are selling, creating a core competence that is hard to replicate. Enterprise Services Architecture enables IT flexibility so that such innovative strategies are practical and affordable.

We will now take a closer look to try to understand the forces putting pressure on business to expose their internal systems to the outside world.

Trends Increasing the Demand for Enterprise Services Architecture

While it is possible to see how expanding automation, increasing flexibility, and so on are beneficial in general, how do we know that they will result in a clear ROI? Why will these factors be an important part of successful companies? In previous eras, expanding to new lines of business, gaining market share, or improving financial stability were the most important factors in determining success. Why are the benefits of Enterprise Services Architecture crucial for the next battles that will be fought in the marketplace?

These questions deserve a book of their own. They cannot be answered in general, but only for a specific company with regard to a specific set of circumstances. The goal of this book is to provide an understanding of Enterprise Services Architecture—its meaning, structure, and implications—so that executives can complete the job of evaluating how Enterprise Services Architecture might help by filling in details from their own context. But, that said, several major trends support the argument that the benefits of Enterprise Services Architecture and composite applications will be key factors for success.

Our argument is that the increase in customer power, direct access to systems, increased competition, and the rise of services will all require increased flexibility in IT systems.

The rise in the power of customers is the first major trend that will drive companies to become more flexible. In many industries, the Internet has shifted the balance of power in favor of customers. In automobile sales, the manufacturer used to control all the information and held all the cards. Consumers who walk into an auto dealer today are likely to be armed with precise cost information that enables them to bargain harder than ever before. With web interfaces for most stores, it is now possible to comparison shop with little effort. The cost of switching suppliers is lower than ever. This consumer power translates into a demand for better service, lower prices, and products more precisely tailored to a much more granular segmentation of the market. This trend places direct demands on the IT infrastructure to support the most customized products and interaction with the consumer at the lowest possible cost.

The second major trend is the rise in computer-mediated interaction with consumers, suppliers, regulators, financial institutions, and every outside party involved in a company's operations. Rickety first-generation web sites have given way to streamlined interfaces that are a pleasure to work with. Companies now differentiate themselves and compete on the basis of user experience. How many of us still use Amazon.com even though we know of discounters that might be able to save us a dollar or two per book at the cost of having to suffer through a more difficult user experience and a less reliable fulfillment process? The rise in interfaces means a rise in the visibility of internal systems. Outsiders can now peer into the glass house of the data center and see if it is a mess. How many companies miss opportunities for meeting customers' needs because they cannot clean up their internal systems well enough to present accurate information to the outside world? This remains a major problem for financial companies that, through internal growth and from mergers, may have the same customer for consumer banking, credit cards, investments, and insurance and not know it. The components of Enterprise Services Architecture can unify this information without requiring extensive retooling of the underlying enterprise applications. The resulting repository of all customer information can provide any particular system access to a complete view of the customer.

Barriers to entry to many businesses are dropping. Small telecommunications providers such as GTE have grown to take on the Baby Bells. Moreover, AOL grew from a small Internet access provider to a giant that gobbled up Time Warner. In the content industry, fierce competition from Internet content providers is leading to rapid consolidation in the publishing industry. Biotech firms are redefining the traditional pharmaceutical industries. As the barriers to entry fall, entrepreneurs and venture capitalists stand ready to take advantage. Peter Drucker points out that new entrants to a business frequently have about a 30 percent cost and efficiency advantage over existing firms because their newly built systems are optimized for the modern supply chain. Companies that are inefficient and inflexible become targets in this environment.

Corporations are seen increasingly by both consumers and other businesses as a set of services. We see interfaces to Amazon.com or Google being exposed as web services. More advanced examples include hosting and support relationships with complex service level agreements. CenterBeam, for example, provides off-site management of a local IT infrastructure. This paradigm exchanges employees for centrally provided services that provide equivalent functionality—maintaining and backing up servers, monitoring important applications, and managing a network. Companies are differentiating themselves from competitors by the kind of services they provide and how they deliver them. The ability of an IT infrastructure to support the delivery of precisely defined services maps naturally to the component structure of Enterprise Services Architecture.

All these trends are leading toward the same transformation in many businesses that occurred in manufacturing. In the automobile industry, for example, the major car manufacturers stopped making many of the components used in their cars. The car makers became the branding and design centers of their industries. Tier 1 suppliers manufacture the components designed to be assembled into completed automobiles. Tier 2 firms make parts that are used to assemble tier 1 components. Tier 3 companies provide raw materials or commodity parts. This manufacturing-style tiering is spreading to a wide variety of industries. Amazon.com, for example, offers used books from thousands of mom-and-pop distributors through the same interface it uses to sell new books. Amazon is happy to do this because it provides better service for its customers and the company makes about the same amount selling a used book from a third party distributor as selling a new book from its warehouse. Amazon.com is the car maker, the assembler or orchestrator, and the smaller bookstores are the tier 1 suppliers. Starbucks, an orchestrator, is becoming a major provider of Wi-Fi services from T-Mobile, a tier 1 company in this scenario.

A fundamental argument of this book is that this sort of tiering will become increasingly important and that Enterprise Services Architecture is the way to be an effective participant in this structure. As we will see in Chapter 6, which addresses where companies should seek to increase their flexibility, the tiering will increasingly force companies to examine what is core to their business and what is secondary. The optimal structure is one in which a company invests its resources in core areas and outsources the rest to other companies whose core competencies lie in those areas. For all this, IT flexibility will be required.

With all of these forces putting pressure on companies to increase flexibility, the question becomes how can the architecture keep up. We will now take a look at the practical next steps.

Transforming the Architecture

Leading innovation in IT can be a risky business. At many companies, the leader of the reengineering effort of the early- to mid-1990s is nowhere to be found. The person who led e-business initiatives was generally fired for not meeting wildly excessive expectations. The leader of the Y2K project is probably not a hero.

"Who is going to believe in anything in this environment?" says Adolf Allesch, a seasoned consultant from Cap Gemini Ernst & Young.

The question is what do you believe and why? The faith that Enterprise Services Architecture requires is as follows:

- The next stage of IT evolution must build on the systems currently in place.

- Architecture must be designed based on a thorough understanding of existing systems and business strategy.

- An architecture based on loosely coupled components and services provides the most flexibility at the lowest cost.

THE EVOLUTION OF IT ARCHITECTURE

- As the cost of change drops in an IT infrastructure, more tactics become affordable, the cost of supporting new relationships is reduced, and new strategies can be implemented faster.

- The ability to change the IT infrastructure faster than competitors to support evolving strategy and to adapt to business conditions will lead to a significant competitive advantage.

The implication of these beliefs is that IT strategy can no longer be decentralized. Even if systems are distributed for operational purposes, they must all speak the same language. Affordable implementation of these articles of faith demands that the IT infrastructure become an ecosystem in which applications present themselves to each other for reuse, where new user interfaces can be constructed out of components and services, and where hard-coded business processes can be replaced with more flexible means of scripting the coordination of components.

Components and services are not a panacea. They can be used to create a monolith (i.e., an inflexible system). But when implementation is guided by a vision for where flexibility is most required and a competent design, Enterprise Services Architecture can be a powerful enabler of business value. Unlike many other technology solutions that provide part of the solution, Enterprise Services Architecture completes the loop and provides an end-to-end vision of cleaning up existing operations and then incorporating third parties. Enterprise Services Architecture provides the essential blueprint for creating systems that allow companies to gain real-time understanding of their operations and take informed actions that produce business advantages. The technical developments that make this possible are the next topic in our analysis.

The Evolution of IT Architecture

While the motivations for bothering with Enterprise Services Architecture at all lay primarily in the realm of business, the reasons that Enterprise Services Architecture has become a short-term imperative lie in the realm of technology.

The design principles of Enterprise Services Architecture spring from mature concepts and techniques such as service-oriented architecture, modeling, and object-oriented programming. Up to this point, these ideas have mostly been relevant to advanced system architects who employed them in creating elegant implementations within applications.

But the expansion of automation throughout the enterprise, the arrival of technologies such as the Internet, XML, web services, and business process management standards, and the maturation of a full set of platform systems for content management, data warehousing, and portals all create the necessary conditions for important architectural ideas to break out of the realm of theory and to start informing the creation of business technology.

Enterprise Services Architecture provides the opportunity to reorganize three generations of business technology around proven architectural principles from computer science. The mainframe era, the client/server era, and the Internet era all filled out the toolbox, creating standards, enterprise applications, and platform component systems to meet the fundamental application and functional needs of the business world. Enterprise Services Architecture now seeks to make sense of it and apply some structure to increase the value businesses can extract from technology.

The reason that Enterprise Services Architecture has gone from a good idea that might happen someday to an exciting opportunity right now is that a variety of elements that have evolved over time are now able to interact in a new way. This is similar to biological evolution in which parts of an organism gradually morph until they all work together differently and enable a major leap forward. Enabling factors in Enterprise Services Architecture's evolutionary process include the availability of advanced development tools, networking standards, and standardized data structures.

The first factor setting the stage for an evolutionary leap is the full suite of enterprise applications developed over the past 30 years. The core financial and control functions were the initial focus of the mainframe era. Applications grew out from this core gradually. During the client/server era, their footprint expanded as applications for Human Resources and Sales Force Automation took root. In the Internet era, the pervasive network allowed applications like Customer Relationship Management, Supply Chain Management and Supplier Relationship Management to automate processes. As a result of these phases, most corporations have collected a heterogeneous mix of applications from many different vendors.

The second major factor in the evolution of infrastructure is the parallel development of platforms and toolkits for a broad scope of application functionality. At the foundation are the operating systems themselves, which provided the base on which computer languages, interactive development environments, and related developer tools were constructed. Relational database systems gradually matured into a stable repository for persistent data from most applications. Platform component systems for content management, data warehousing, and application integration all provided powerful toolkits to build custom applications and extend the functionality of existing legacy and enterprise applications.

A third development that makes Enterprise Services Architecture ready for prime time is the way the Internet broke through the armor that surrounded the enterprise. With TCP/IP as the standard way of communicating across networks, web browsers based on HTML as the user interface, and HTTP as the communication protocol, enterprise applications could now reach out directly to consumers and suppliers. Applications could also more easily communicate with each other. The investment boom that grew from these technological developments resulted in the acceleration of the growth in enterprise applications and platform component systems. Network-oriented enterprise applications and platform components such as application servers and enterprise application integration (EAI) systems were created in this period.

Data is being prepared for Enterprise Services Architecture through XML. Inspired by the simplicity and popularity of HTML, the ornate and complicated language of SGML was distilled into XML, a flexible way to describe the structure of data. XML also describes interfaces and protocols in a way that is interoperable across different applications and platforms. The rise of XML spurred a wave of standard setting for data and protocols in almost every industry that continues to this day. Efforts like RosettaNet and OASIS are extending standards in every direction including the semantics of the data. Almost every standards effort is based on XML in one way or another. Enterprise applications use XML as a standard way of describing data, and EAI technology moves XML messages from one application to another. XML has also spurred the creation of a variety of toolkits for managing and transforming data stored in XML format. The result of the spread of XML is that conversations about standardization and integration are much more focused on what to do rather than how to do it.

While all these other developments are profound in their effect, web services is perhaps the most significant. It is the catalyst that allows Enterprise Services Architecture to spring into being. Web services are like a universal plug and socket system that allows applications to describe and implement different ways to communicate with each other. Unlike CORBA or DCOM and other previous attempts at this sort of connector technology, web services are based on XML and truly platform-independent protocols such as SOAP. Like HTML and XML, web services are also simple and flexible. Web services technology has become the default interface to application components and services. Web services are simple and universal enough that the vast majority of the participants in the IT universe are convinced that all applications will eventually be able to communicate with each other through web services. This simplicity has become a problem as its popularity has outstripped its maturity. Some basic definitions for security, guaranteed delivery of messages, transactions, and other portions of the standard are still being defined. These gaps do not obscure the fact that, like XML, web services have changed the conversation about application integration to focus more on the goals than the methods.

One development that is still more a hope than a reality is the emergence of a strong consensus around the creation of languages to describe business processes. IBM and Microsoft combined their separate long-standing efforts toward business process modeling to create a common language called BPEL4WS, which merges the best ideas from both companies. SAP has signed on as an author of the standard and many other leading technology vendors also endorse BPEL4WS. Similar efforts called Business Process Modeling Language and Web Service Choreography Interface are also under development. These languages could become a standard way to describe the orchestration of components and services and the foundation for portable descriptions of business processes. The largest benefit accrues from these efforts if one of these languages becomes the standardized way to control the behavior of enterprise applications, which would allow tremendous configurability and interoperability.

With all of this infrastructure in place, including a complete set of functionality from enterprise applications and platform component systems, standard ways of describing data and interfaces between applications, and even possibly a method of orchestrating the behavior of multiple components, Enterprise Services Architecture is now a practical possibility. The amount of work required to achieve a better architecture has become manageable.

Inside Enterprise Services Architecture

So far we have explained the context in which Enterprise Services Architecture exists and the business benefits that may accrue. We have hinted at the mechanisms, such as loosely coupled components, services, and modeling, that represent crucial building blocks. Now we will delve into the moving parts and demonstrate how they work together.

It is fashionable to complain about silos of data trapped in distinct enterprise applications, as if this problem could have been foreseen and avoided. Perhaps it could have, but during the boom times from 1995 to 2000 when most of these applications were implemented, few companies kept their eye on creating a coherent architecture. Technology vendors provided little assistance during this period as they too focused on expanding the footprint of application functionality rather than on the larger issues of integration. Implementing applications to attack new markets and pave the way for growth was the order of the day. Most companies preferred gaining the automation from new applications to reconciling and synchronizing all the data and functionality. The result was the silos: each new application arriving with new data and new functionality, separate from those that came before.

While all of this may be obvious, the best way to escape the silos is far from clear. As the IT industry matures, it will be beneficial for products and systems to follow the same road as manufacturing and become a series of subsystems or components. How can a company or a vendor figure out the right collection of components? How will they fit together? What benefits would accrue from such a structure? What problems would arise? How will they be purchased or constructed? And at what cost?

Economic reality sets limits on any solution. Investment in the current generation of systems and the value they provide is so large that we cannot start from scratch. How can we build on top of the current generation of applications in an incremental fashion? How can the company rise above the silos to get flexibility at a reasonable cost?

To explain in concrete terms the solution Enterprise Services Architecture proposes, we will take a brief tour through the development of enterprise applications from the mainframe era to the present day.

The first computer applications that gained wide acceptance were built on mainframe computers that had only the minimal support for development in the operating system. The resulting applications had to do everything for themselves in one big monolithic blob of functionality as shown in Figure 1-1.

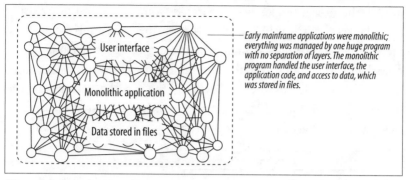

Early mainframe applications were monolithic; everything was managed by one huge program with no separation of layers. The monolithic program handled the user interface, the application code, and access to data, which was stored in files.

Figure 1-1. Monolithic application structure

Monolithic applications fulfill the purpose for which they were originally constructed but they are hard to adapt and improve. The layers, to the extent they exist at all, are tightly connected to each other. A small change in one area can break the entire application.

The next step for application architecture involved separating the database from the monolithic application, creating a two-tier application. The user interface and the application code remained entwined in the monolith, as shown in Figure 1-2. This structure took advantage of database programs that started to arrive as separate products.

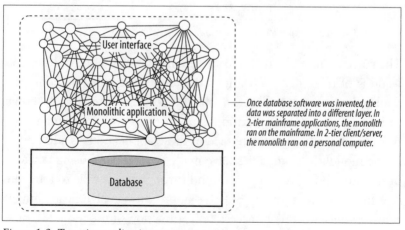

Once database software was invented, the data was separated into a different layer. In 2-tier mainframe applications, the monolith ran on the mainframe. In 2-tier client/server, the monolith ran on a personal computer.

Figure 1-2. Two-tier application structure

In the late 1980s and early 1990s, with the help of the personal computer and the network, the three-tier application arrived. In this model, the user interface was separated from the monolith, creating three layers as shown in Figure 1-3. Both the user interface and the monolithic application would sometimes run on a personal computer, and sometimes only the user interface would run there. After the arrival of the Internet, everything ran on the server and the browser became the interface. The monolith still existed but shrank as the user interface layer was carved out.

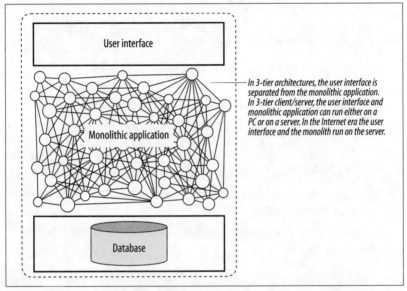

User interface

Monolithic application

In 3-tier architectures, the user interface is separated from the monolithic application. In 3-tier client/server, the user interface and monolithic application can run either on a PC or on a server. In the Internet era the user interface and the monolith run on the server.

Database

Figure 1-3. Three-tier application structure

The current architecture at most companies is now composed of collections of three-tier applications that either use personal computer applications or web browsers as the primary user interface, as shown in Figure 1-4. These applications are the silos and the fundamental problem is that the user interface of these applications is still bound to the monolith. Companies have made progress in reusing portions of the monolith through portals and through using APIs to integrate one monolith to another. But this approach has significant limitations. Portals are able to access only a fraction of the monolith, and integration using APIs is difficult and expensive.

The primary goal of Enterprise Services Architecture is to overcome these limitations so that creating new applications is much easier

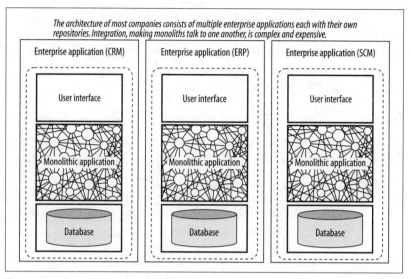

Figure 1-4. Current enterprise architecture

and much more of the monolithic functionality may be reused. This is achieved by breaking the monolith into components as shown in Figure 1-5.

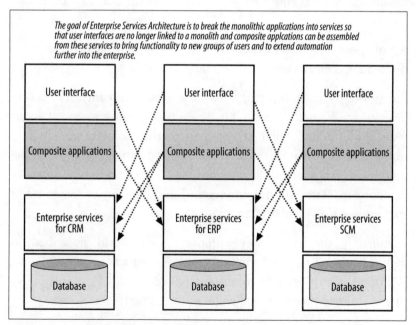

Figure 1-5. Enterprise Services Architecture

Many important things are shown in this diagram. First of all, the monolithic portion of the application has been transformed into a set of components that are connected through services that hide the complexity of components from one another. This unlocks value by making much more of the application reusable.

User interfaces have been freed from the monolith and are not limited by what the original designer of the monolithic application thought was required years ago. They are bound instead to the tasks users need to perform their work and participate in processes. Components can be used to support as many user interfaces as make sense and each user interface can draw on components from several different enterprise applications.

This structure also allows composite applications to be constructed. New components can be created and combined with components from existing enterprise applications to solve new problems and automate processes without regard to the limitations of silos. Integration between applications or with outside parties also becomes component-based and can be accomplished much quicker and cheaper.

All of these benefits accrue when the monoliths have been transformed into components.

But before we get too joyful, let's come down to reality. The world described in Figure 1-5 is not possible with current versions of enterprise applications, which still present their monolithic functionality through APIs. It is impossible for us to build architectures assuming that every enterprise application has been reconstituted into a set of components. They are not and won't look like that for five years or so, by some reasonable estimates.

Fortunately the completely componentized world described in Figure 1-5 is not required for extraction of significant business value. We don't need flexibility in absolutely every part of the infrastructure in order to meet the challenges of the marketplace.

Because of this, we also do not need to wait five years to get the benefit of a componentized architecture. The Enterprise Services Architecture platform, a layer of software that allows components to be constructed from the current generation of enterprise applications, allows us to introduce the right level of flexibility to create maximum value, as shown in Figure 1-6.

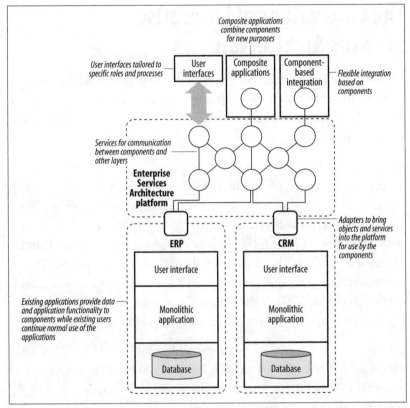

Figure 1-6. Enterprise Services Architecture platform structure

In this graphic, adapters bring the functionality of enterprise applications into a component architecture that can be used to help create new user interfaces, composite applications, or integrations. Some applications such as payroll are stable. Some applications are flexible or dynamic and it is in these areas where change and optimization will occur. This is where components are needed. In Chapter 6, we examine in detail how to determine where flexibility is required in an architecture to provide maximum business value.

This structure brings up a large design problem. What is the right size and shape for the components we have been referring to? How must they be constructed to produce the value we claim? We will now examine the fundamental principles by which these questions are properly answered.

The Core Values of Enterprise Services Architecture

The core values of Enterprise Services Architecture can be expressed in terms from the realm of computer science. The ideas behind these words, however, are not impenetrable or difficult to understand. They are around us every day.

All of the fundamental ideas of Enterprise Services Architecture are simple, but we have mathematical-sounding names for them: abstraction, models, components, objects, services, processes, loose coupling. Enterprise Services Architecture is at its core the systematic application of principles of successful design applied to IT architecture to produce the maximum benefits for a business. Like a manufacturing company, we want to have flexibility in what products we build with the lowest possible cost for design, manufacturing, and maintenance. A simple example will help to illustrate.

Let's start with the old joke that goes like this: if you ask him what time it is, he will tell you how to build a watch. When we ask our hypothetical friend for the time, let's freeze the action before he answers and think about what we are asking. Time itself is a standard abstraction. Seconds, minutes, and hours do not exist anywhere except in our minds. Time passes; that's reality. But the way we keep track is a convention. There are 60 seconds in a minute and 60 minutes in a hour. Would time be more useful if there were 100 seconds in a minute and 100 minutes in an hour and 10 hours each day, with 5 being the equivalent of noon? Who cares? Our current division of time happened so long ago that it isn't really practical to change it. Time is time, and we are so used to it that we think of it as a reality, not an abstraction. It doesn't really make sense to change the way we mark time because it would be so impractical.

Now let's start the action back up again, and let our friend answer the question. He telling us how to build a watch instead of what time it is. He tells us about the ticking mechanism that records that small increments of time have passed and how the counters add those small increments together and register seconds, minutes, and hours. He is telling us more than we need to know and is not telling us what we want to know. We want our friend to hide the complexity of the workings of his watch from us and just provide the useful information that is important to us. Hiding the details is what happens in an abstraction. The complex workings of the watch proceed inside the abstraction but the useful information, the time, pops out.

Hiding complexity, making a two-sided conversation simpler, reducing the conversation to the important elements is the essence of abstraction. The first core value of Enterprise Services Architecture is to increase abstraction where it makes business sense.

The second core value of Enterprise Services Architecture is modularity. The strategy is to manage the complexity of a large system by breaking it into a number of smaller parts. Each part should contain enough functionality to do some useful portion of the work of the system.

The third core value of Enterprise Services Architecture is to connect the modular parts (the components) using services. A service is a description of a specific interface to a component that performs some function. A service for customer lookup might take last name and first name as input parameters and return a list of customers who match. The description of what can be asked of a component is a service interface. The code inside the component that does the work is a service implementation.

The fourth core value of Enterprise Services Architecture is loose coupling. Loose coupling means that the service interface exposes as little as possible of the service implementation. The complex work done by the service implementation should not be visible to the outside world. Hiding such complexity makes reusing the component much easier and reduces to a minimum the unnecessary dependencies that make a monolithic architecture hard to change.

The final core value of Enterprise Services Architecture is an emphasis on design that is incrementally improved. At the beginning of the creation of a set of components, the architect must sort out all of the functions of an application and then decide which services each component should have and how they will all work together to get the work done. In a typical design, some components orchestrate the work of other components. Some components represent important data such as the customer object. Other components may manage a resource such as an RFID scanner that reads information about products. No matter how much time is spent on a design, generally new requirements come up after implementation. It is the philosophy of Enterprise Services Architecture that the design process should continue based on what is learned in implementation so that the system is gradually improved.

Let's return to our watch example. Making the watch into a component would be the equivalent of hiding the inner workings and only allowing a predefined set of questions to be asked. What time is it? What date is it? What day of the week is it? These three questions represent services of the component. The inner workings of the watch are no longer important. The watch has been modeled as a set of three services. The inner workings should be able to be replaced as long as those services are provided. The complexity of the watch is still there, but there is now something in between, an abstraction that reduces the watch into three services.

The goal of these core values is to create a complex of components that have the minimum dependencies among them so that they can be recombined for different purposes with minimal effort. The other end of the spectrum is a monolithic system, which is not broken into modules and has many dependencies. We have spent a significant amount of energy trashing monoliths. Now we will explain why we do not like them.

Shortcomings of Monolithic Architecture

In the context of Enterprise Services Architecture, monolithic means one time, one purpose, one way.

Most companies do not have architectures that adhere to Enterprise Services Architecture principles and they suffer for it in a variety of ways. A nest of enterprise applications that evolved without a plan tends toward unmanageable complexity. It is possible to increase automation in such an environment, but the cost is high and every additional integration increases maintenance costs and reduces flexibility.

How do monoliths make companies suffer? Tight coupling makes change expensive or impossible. Products cannot be upgraded to take advantage of the next version. The IT staff is fearful to change anything because they don't know what will break. Integrations are expensive and always start from scratch. Functionality is not reused. The answer to enabling a new business strategy is no, not yes.

How are monoliths built? First, build a solution as fast as possible without regard to flexibility or future needs. Add functionality a bit at a time. Voilà—in no time you will have trouble changing the system or adding anything to it. Vinod Khosla, a venture capitalist with Kleiner, Perkins, Caufield, & Byers, likes to illustrate monolithic architecture with the image of the Cat in the Hat balancing 20 different objects while standing on top of a ball.

The problem with current integrations between applications can be described perfectly using the watch example. Tightly coupled integrations involve looking at the complex workings of the watch on both sides, understanding them, and then building a bridge between them. Such connections are fragile and expensive to build and maintain. If the inner workings of one of the watches change, it may have a dramatic effect on many integrations. Complexity on one side mapped directly to complexity on the other side is the essence of tight coupling. The more dependencies between the two sides, the tighter the coupling. The more that one side needs to keep track of what is going on in the other side, the tighter the coupling. In tight coupling, the impact of a change on one side is hard to predict. One has to know a lot before one can make even the simplest change.

The classic mistake that is repeated over and over in unplanned architectures is tight coupling to the data model. When a CRM system tries to read data from the HR system, the tightly coupled method reads the database directly. If there is a change in the database structure that affects what is being read, the program reading the data must be changed. However, the person upgrading the HR system may not know that the CRM system now depends on the HR system having a certain database structure. The new schema in HR will have consequences for CRM, a problem that may be uncovered during testing but probably won't be found until the new version is in production.

As the number of such dependencies increases, it may become impractical and costly to upgrade an enterprise application from one version to another. Taking advantage of new opportunities to integrate with suppliers or offering direct access to customers can be difficult. Reusing portions of an application is difficult when the functionality of the enterprise is trapped in large monolithic chunks. Composite applications, one of the main advantages of Enterprise Services Architecture that we will explain in detail below, are expensive to build in this context and only add to the complexity and inflexibility.

The worst effect of a rigid, inflexible, and expensive to maintain architecture may be the way that it shuts down innovation and creativity. When people are fearful of changing anything because the unintended consequences may be so devastating, they are unlikely to propose new ways of doing business that require system changes.

Components and Services

Components and services are the cure for monolithic architecture. Given the previous discussion, Enterprise Services Architecture can be described simply as a path away from a tightly coupled, monolithic architecture toward one that is loosely coupled and based on components and services. The key challenge is deciding what components to create, what services they should offer, and how they should be connected. To explore these issues, we will take a look at the structure of enterprise applications.

In a company of almost any size, enterprise applications are the fundamental building blocks. All have a similar structure that is generally described through the following layers of the application stack:

User interface layer
> Manages communication with the user

Process layer
> Keeps track of where the user is in the process, and orchestrates the work of the services and objects to get the work done

Services layer
> Performs the work of the application by extracting data from objects, performing some useful function, and then returning the result

Object layer
> Contains the objects that are collections of data and services for maintaining and performing basic transformations on the data

Persistence layer
> Stores the data from the objects

These layers are illustrated in Figure 1-7.

Components, which are constructed out of these elements, consist of objects, services, and processes that are related to each other. Generally, a component aggregates many of these elements and communicates with the outside world through a simplified set of services that constitute the abstraction of the component. The scope of a component can be very large or quite small. Several applications might work together to provide one component. A single application might be broken into many different components. One component might create a unified view of what's going on in many components.

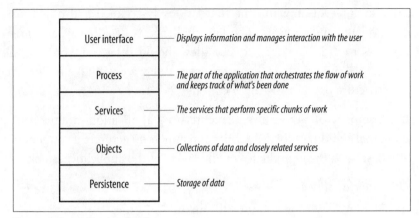

Figure 1-7. Application Stack

Services connect one component to another and exist at many levels. The methods on objects can be thought of as services. A web service that allows a name lookup can be a service. An enterprise service may be an aggregation of a set of web services that performs a common function such as controlling the process of creating a new customer record.

One of the key questions that this book attempts to answer is how to sort out the elements of a firm's infrastructure and decide where and at what level of granularity components should be defined.

So what are the core values of Enterprise Services Architecture? Enterprise Services Architecture is in favor of increasing abstraction, componentization, and loose coupling using services, all under the umbrella of a comprehensive and incrementally evolving design. Enterprise Services Architecture is against monolithic aggregation of functionality, tight coupling, and unmanageable complexity. Enterprise Services Architecture seeks to create practical business advantages rather than uniformity or consistency for its own sake.

Seasoned technologists and businesspeople will have had enough of this discussion by now, even if they are sold on the core values of Enterprise Services Architecture. As the old pros know well, "better" in the world of IT does not mean technology that has a more prestigious computer science pedigree or a more perfectly designed abstraction. The best technology from an IT perspective produces the most business value and helps a company win in the market-place. We now turn to the issue of whether the core values of Enter-prise Services Architecture can get that job done.

The Business Value of Enterprise Services Architecture

The starting point for Enterprise Services Architecture at most com-panies is a relatively large base of application functionality. In the past 10 years, enterprise applications have extended automation to parts of the organization that previously did not have support for their operations. The mainframe era focused on centralized applica-tions for financial information. Customer relationship management, sales force automation, and supply chain management barely existed. Now that enterprise applications have extended their reach throughout the enterprise, the new direction for automation is across the existing applications.

The new functionality added as a company implements Enterprise Services Architecture will likely be composed of parts from existing systems and will focus on the following goals:

- Automation of cross-functional processes that span the bound-aries of the organization and of existing systems

- Support for strategic processes that require flexible workflows and integration of collaboration and unstructured information—such as documents and spreadsheets—with transactional sys-tems for finance and operations

- Expansion of the existing user base for enterprise applications within the organization by extending access and improving sup-port for specific roles through focused user interfaces

- Tighter integration with systems of suppliers and key partners

- Direct access for customers, suppliers, and key partners

- Increased support for targeting specific market niches

- Improvement of change management processes such as mergers and acquisitions or program management

This new frontier for automation will provide important benefits. Companies will gather more data, think faster, and integrate decisions with actions. The flexibility of the IT infrastructure will allow companies to reinvent their businesses with less cost and to extend their value network more cheaply.

While all of these goals could theoretically be met with existing technology, as a practical matter, the integrations turn out to be brittle and expensive and they are tightly coupled in a way that we will explain later in this chapter. Tightly coupled means that developers who build integrations between enterprise applications of the kind shown in Figure 1-8 must understand all of the complexity of the monolithic enterprise applications being connected. This prerequisite increases the expense and reduces the flexibility of the integration.

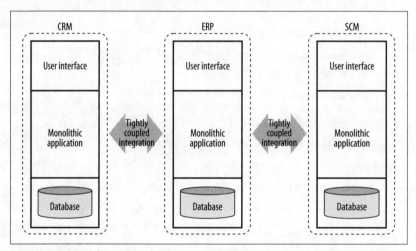

Figure 1-8. Typical enterprise architecture

Composite Applications

One new type of system built on this architecture is called composite applications. Packaged Composite Applications sit on top of an Enterprise Services Architecture platform layer, a software product that creates components out of existing enterprise applications. *Packaged Composite Applications* (O'Reilly), the first book in this series, explored the nature and implications of the composite applications paradigm.

One of the most important aspects of Enterprise Services Architecture is the new kind of automation that composite applications enable and make affordable. Because a composite application sits on top of all of the existing applications that have been made into components, it now can ignore the boundaries between the underlying applications. Indeed, they may not even be visible to the composite applications. This cross-functional automation of processes easily spans application boundaries. Components from transactional systems that keep track of records in databases can be combined with components that manage unstructured information found in documents, email, and discussion groups. Collaborative activity of a wide group of people such as email, discussion forums, or file sharing can be centralized and coordinated. New relationships between information from a diverse set of underlying applications can be managed and stored.

The component-based applications structures we explain below provide examples of how components in Enterprise Services Architecture help create each type of application.

For example, companies will think faster because, by nature, composite applications rapidly assemble critical information for strategic decisions. Composite applications can reach through components provided by an Enterprise Services Architecture platform into the distinct enterprise applications, pulling out the information needed to describe the current state of a company's business. Instead of having to wait days or weeks for manual rollups, composite applications can make this happen instantly, and more effort can be spent analyzing decisions than gathering information. Composite applications also facilitate distributing and collaborating on strategic information (see Figure 1-9).

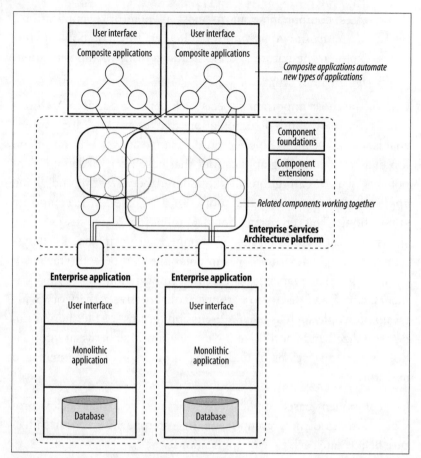

Figure 1-9. Composite applications

When decisions have been reached and action needs to be taken, composite applications built on an Enterprise Services Architecture platform go beyond read-only views of information in a variety of systems. The components built on top of existing systems can allow invocation of functionality in the underlying systems. If information in a sales order is found to be incorrect, a user doesn't have to then go to the system of record and find the data field in question. Corrections can be made immediately from the composite application at the time of discovery. A variety of underlying enterprise applications can be invoked and coordinated from a composite application.

Enterprise Services Architecture also increases the instrumentation of a business. The number of available metrics increases, as does the ease of getting them. Components organized to implement an order fulfillment process can provide reporting at each step of the process. When such a process is implemented in a tightly coupled set of objects within a monolithic legacy or enterprise application, information about the process is limited. Legacy systems provide coarse-grained information, usually just the time the order was started and the time it was completed. In a component-based composite application, the metrics are more granular and include details such as the time required to take the order, the time it took to prepare the order for production, the time it took to assemble all the parts needed to fill the order, the time it took to prepare the order for shipping, and so on. Better information highlights inefficiency and drives out politically motivated finger-pointing.

When it comes to supporting new supplier relationships, the components of the composite application provide a clean level of abstraction for the automation of the relationship as shown in Figure 1-10. Suppliers in essence become defined as a component. Supporting new relationships requires designing the component and determining what objects will be managed within it and what services will be used to represent the supplier relationship. The component may be implemented within the boundaries of a company's IT infrastructure or remotely. (Web services, which we discuss later, make implementing remote components easier than ever before.) Supplier relationships are commonly automated using EDI technology in which an agreed upon document format is transferred between two companies and carries the information needed to support the relationship. Although transferring documents back and forth is a powerful technique for coordinating the behavior of systems at both companies, it is a paradigm that smacks of the world of batch processing. In a world in which applications are facing customers or highly paid staff instead of data entry clerks, users need real-time links to corporate business partners, a crucial benefit of the component-based approach. Imagine if Amazon.com could not tell for sure if a book was available but had to get back to you later after the EDI messages had a chance to flow back and forth between companies. Supplier relationships are increasingly trending in this direction.

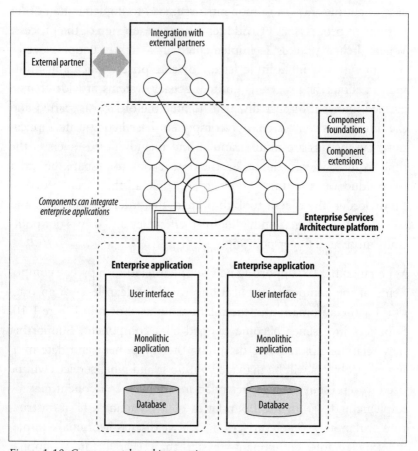

Figure 1-10. Component-based integration

Composite applications expand the reach of the underlying enterprise applications to new populations of users, as illustrated in Figure 1-11. The typical enterprise application is primarily transactional, meaning that records in databases that represent specific financial or organizational transformations are the focus of the application. An order for a product or hiring a new employee are classic examples. The users that interact with these applications are primarily administrative staff with specialized roles. In a composite application world enabled by an Enterprise Services Architecture platform, components from all different sorts of applications can be reassembled to meet the needs of a broader cross-section of a company. As a result of expanding the reach of the application, more people in a company get the benefit of the information and the functionality of the underlying enterprise application. This increased reach is enabled because the components span the available information and functionality, but also because development is affordable. The cost of assembling a new composite application is much lower than creating a traditional application. Assembling services from a set of components is much more productive and less expensive to maintain than creating a traditional application with languages like Java or C#. Using a process-modeling approach to configure the behavior of an application or to orchestrate many components offers the possibility of even more flexibility. Process modeling is a method of controlling the behavior of an application in a simplified manner that is much less difficult and expensive than programming.

The lower cost of assembling applications is not merely a matter of development efficiency. When the cost of automation is lower, so is the cost of creating customized products or services to address a market niche, which can be a significant factor in increasing the number of niches that can be profitably addressed.

Composite applications also improve on existing enterprise applications through support for processes with a fuzzy definition. Automation of a process in traditional enterprise applications tends to be rigid. The automation of cross-functional and strategic processes tends to focus on processes that are less precisely defined than the process of filling an order. Making a decision about an M&A transaction, for example, involves identifying potential target companies, evaluating their suitability for acquisition, narrowing down the list to a smaller set of targets, negotiating the transaction, performing due diligence, and then executing the merger. Each of these steps involves information gathering and analysis by a large group of people inside and outside the company. Parts of the process may be rigid while other parts may involve tracking the collaboration in documents, email, discussion lists, and video conferences. Part of the

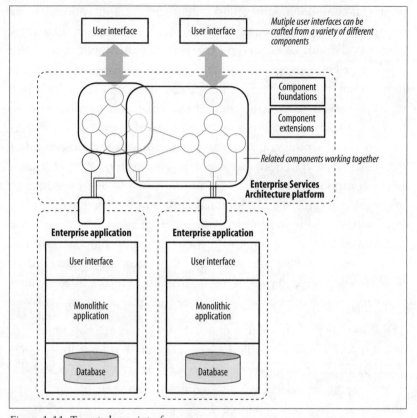

Figure 1-11. Targeted user interfaces

information for a merger resides in transactional applications while other parts are found in unstructured documents and spreadsheets. Composite applications' ability to automate the backbone of a process and fill in the gaps with collaborative functionality greatly expands the potential footprint of automation.

These beneficial factors are the mechanisms of change that result in greater flexibility, an increased scope of tactics, reduced cost of change, and the expansion of automation in an era of composite applications based on Enterprise Services Architecture platform components.

An example from the beverage industry puts many of Enterprise Services Architecture's benefits into perspective. A global beverage maker started noticing that dance clubs accounted for a significant proportion of its sales. It turned out that one of their specialty spirit drinks was being mixed with a soft drink to create soda pop with a kick. After studying the market, the company determined that there was a niche opportunity to sell a premixed version of the drink to a small but significant population. The problem was that it would never work out financially if the company addressed the market in traditional ways because their traditional marketing and distribution cost structure was based on launching a nationwide product with a potentially massive audience, not a niche market.

To address the market, the beverage company created a streamlined process that involved tighter and lower-cost coordination with their advertising agencies and other marketing support firms and an altered relationship with their distributors that allowed for smaller quantities to affordably move through the supply chain. To automate this process from beginning to end, all parties had to adopt a more efficient Internet-based automation of the advertising and marketing programs and move smaller quantities through the distribution system. As a result, a market niche was served with a targeted product. Further, the company put processes in place that would open up other niche markets. This transformation is similar to the way that composite applications allow companies to serve smaller niches of users because such applications are cheaper to create and maintain.

Process and Compliance in Implementation

It has always made sense to have a long-term vision for corporate IT architecture. In the past, this vision has taken the form of presentations that explain "where we are going." Frequently these slides are so vague that it is impossible to disagree with them ("We are going someplace good"). In other cases, the plan stretches out for 10 years or more, making the vision so distant that it is ignored ("It will take a long time to get where we are going"). Enterprise Services Architecture transforms this nebulous cloud of architectural intention into a much more specific set of steps that allow a company to determine how far away each of its systems is from the desired level of compo-nentization. Enterprise Services Architecture makes it quite clear exactly how we will get "where we are going" and provides milestones for progress along the way.

The Enterprise Services Architecture Process

For most of the history of IT, the primary goal has been internal efficiency. The current generation of enterprise applications are precisely aimed at that goal. The next wave of change for IT will be driven by an increasing demand that companies work better with the marketplace, as Andy Mulholland points out in the Afterword to this book.

Whether a company believes that Enterprise Services Architecture is a good idea or not, its IT house will have to be in order to take advantage of advanced interaction with suppliers. However a company believes that it will thrive and grow, its IT strategy will need to be tightly synchronized with its business goals. It is at this juncture, between the synchronization of business and IT strategy, where most architectural plans fail.

The mistakes are varied but numerous and deserve a book of their own. But to get the plan right, the company must have complete and justified answers to a variety of questions:

- Where should we be on the technology curve? Should we be using the most advanced, bleeding-edge technology or should we be using the most stable, proven technology?
- What is our core competency? How and where are we differentiating ourselves from the competition?
- What changes are taking place in our marketplace and how are we planning to adapt our systems to meet new challenges?
- What are the most stable and the most volatile parts of our business and how will our IT systems support the needs of each part?

These basic questions are just a start and Enterprise Services Architecture is silent on all of them. Enterprise Services Architecture has nothing to say about what a company's core competency is or where it should be on the technology curve. Enterprise Services Architecture comes into play after you answer the last two questions about the marketplace and the stability of various parts of the company. Once a company decides where it is likely to need flexibility, integration with external partners, and optimized processes, Enterprise Services Architecture provides a way to get there.

Chapter 6 provides detailed discussion of these issues, but here's a high-level view of the game plan. Imagine that each system in your architecture is a component and define what services it provides, what data it owns, and how it interacts with other systems. When analyzed in this way, some systems will be just fine as they are. A payroll system, perhaps one that is outsourced, is probably just perfect as a component in its current state. Information describing what everyone should be paid is fed in, and checks and tax calculations emerge. Most companies will not find a strategic advantage in changing this.

A thorough analysis of existing systems reveals the important data elements that exist in multiple locations as well as the systems that will support the company in an evolving marketplace or in meeting changing customer needs. Where flexibility and optimization can be anticipated, Enterprise Services Architecture's component approach can lower the cost of change. Where customization of enterprise applications or the construction of new customized applications is required, using the Enterprise Services Architecture component approach can dramatically increase the value and usefulness of this investment. Some components will be large, and Enterprise Services Architecture provides an ecosystem so that the services they provide can be reused and recombined to create new composite applications to extend automation to strategic and cross-functional processes. Enterprise Services Architecture ensures that every step in "where we are going" provides more power to the enterprise and increased business value. Every dollar spent on Enterprise Services Architecture should put a company further ahead of its competition and in a position to more completely leverage existing technology.

The key to proper application of Enterprise Services Architecture is finding the few processes that are likely to be in need of componentization. Key data objects that show up over and over number in the tens, not the hundreds. Companies rarely try to differentiate themselves in every aspect of their operations. Enterprise Services Architecture provides the structure so that investment in flexibility can be focused on a certain aspect of a company's operations in a way that allows the finer-grained components to work in conjunction with macro-level components. The Enterprise Services Architecture blueprint provides a way for this focus to shift over time with minimum disruption and maximum reuse.

If a company's judgment about itself is correct and it invests in the right sort of componentization, it should result in a good position from which successful combinations will result.

Compliance

The notion of Enterprise Services Architecture compliance makes objective analysis possible. Enterprise Services Architecture compliance is a hierarchy of abstraction that can be applied to any individual system, to a group of systems, or to a company's architecture as a whole. Each level of Enterprise Services Architecture compliance is a defined by a combination of how completely a company understands what it wants from a system and how well that system is able to deliver it. Much of the time when we say *system*, we will actually be talking about one application, although a system could be comprised of many applications working together or could be a part of an application. By *objects*, we mean data and closely related services.

The levels of Enterprise Services Architecture compliance are:

Level 1: The Big Think
   Understanding and documenting the important data, objects, services, and processes that a system provides.

Level 2: Data Services

Read/write access to the objects of the system in a way that maintains the consistency of the application.

Level 3: User Interface Abstraction

The ability to separate the user interface from the rest of the system so that the services can be used as components in composite user interfaces or by other systems.

Level 4: Loosely Coupled Components and Services

The services and objects are grouped into components that are designed so that they can be loosely coupled.

Level 5: Process Control

Processes are exposed and configurable to allow the behavior of a component to be easily changed.

The purpose of this scale is to assist in categorizing what sort of componentization is needed for different parts of a company's architecture. Applying Enterprise Services Architecture is the process of understanding where your business is likely to need the agility, flexibility, and reduced costs of integration and change that result from increasing abstraction through a componentized architecture.

In Chapters 4 and 5, we closely examine what each of these levels means and how the levels relate to the current state of enterprise application systems. In Chapter 6, we analyze different ways of deciding on the right Enterprise Services Architecture compliance level for each of your systems, and in Chapter 7 we provide a road map for execution.

It is reasonable, and perhaps wise, to be skeptical of the value of this sort of componentization. Flexibility for its own sake is a losing proposition. In the next section, we will review the process of how a company should analyze where the componentization of Enterprise Services Architecture might make sense, but before we do, an example from the history of SAP might help illustrate the value of the clean separation of layers that Enterprise Services Architecture is all about.

In the early 1990s, SAP was completing a four-year project in which its R/2 ERP system was being rewritten to take advantage of the more advanced partitioning capabilities of IMS and to further extend the functionality of the suite. SAP applications are separated into the application code, which is written in the ABAP fourth generation language, and the Basis layer, which is a componentization of the services provided by the operating system and database. The development of the R/3 Basis layer had been taking place on Unix workstations and was going to be ported over to the IBM systems. The ABAP development of the R/3 applications was taking place on the IBM mainframes. The plan was to move the R/3 Basis layer to the IBM systems to complete development of R/3. When the debugging began, it turned out that the development tools on the IBM systems had some severe limitations that prevented any sort of progress. The practical power of abstraction revealed itself.

Peter Zencke, a senior SAP executive who is now a member of the executive board, suggested that instead of moving the Basis code from Unix to IBM, why not move the ABAP code from IBM to Unix? The fact that debugging could proceed then on Unix would allow the company to show R/3 at the upcoming Hanover Fair which was only six weeks away. Many long nights later, this approach proved successful. The availability of R/3 on Unix transformed SAP and— along with many other features of the software and the breadth of the range of its applications—set the stage for the company's dramatic growth in the rest of the 1990s.

The lesson related to Enterprise Services Architecture is the flexibility that a cleanly defined abstraction gave to SAP to pursue a completely new business strategy. If the layers had been intertwined or tightly coupled to IBM software, then SAP would be much a smaller company than it is today.

An Industry Grows Up

The next step for the IT industry is the componentization of applications. Componentization will occur gradually as vendors figure out the right way to use web services and all of the other standards and tools at their disposal to create components out of their products that can meet the needs of their customers.

The IT industry currently faces the end of a youthful period in which each era opened virgin frontiers for enterprise applications or functional platform component systems. Dynamic change and innovation, of course, will still occur, but the existing footprint of IT infrastructure is so large that the first question that any new technology will have to answer is how well it works with existing systems. We look at how the maturation of the industry will affect technology vendors, the enterprise value chain, and the world at large in Chapters 8 and 9.

The forces driving standardization will result in a new battle for standards followed by a continuing wave of commoditization. For example, the initial conflict will relate to which vendor will define the basic components that present the functionality of an application such as corporate accounting. Once one or two vendors have proven dominant, all other related applications will write their software to address the winning component and service models. Other vendors will then imitate the standard components, which could lead to commoditization of the applications.

Vendors will expand their functionality to combat commoditization, but for mature applications, this will prove difficult. Once corporate accounting has been defined in a well-designed set of components, there is no longer significant functionality to add as a differentiator.

Vendors will instead differentiate themselves with either comprehensive component offerings that meet a wide variety of generic business needs or with offerings that effectively target a vertical market. Companies that provide component breadth or depth will become the equivalent of manufacturers. More than that, they will become service integrators. They will outsource more of the standardized processes, aggregate component services from multiple vendors, and package them in the form of innovative customer solutions. They will have a sophisticated understanding of the components they need to support their core processes, will purchase or outsource those that are commodities, and will create a flexible system of components to allow strategic flexibility, optimization of the value chain, and customization of products and services to serve specific customer needs. In other words, the companies that succeed will understand how to map their business needs from the IT infrastructure onto a set of components.

The goal of this book is to provide a thorough explanation of Enterprise Services Architecture, to convey a useful way to think about the deeper problems of enterprise computing, and to teach companies how to chart the course from where they are to a place that opens up a powerful sequence of moves that translate into success. Chapter 2 illustrates this architectural paradigm with some examples of Enterprise Services Architecture in action.

2

In Practice

The examples of applied technology in this chapter are designed to take Enterprise Services Architecture out of the realm of theory and show how concepts like abstraction, components, services, and loose coupling are realized on the IT battlefield.

We look at five different applications that vary in complexity and scope. All of the examples have made a significant impact and also illustrate one or more principles of Enterprise Services Architecture.

The examples are:

- A supply chain automation system that shows how components allow a distributed and outsourced complex of suppliers and manufacturers to be managed as if they were all the part of the same company

- A plant maintenance system that improves the efficiency and quality of the process of maintaining and optimizing the performance of complex and expensive equipment

- An extension to ERP applications that allows idle assets to be put up for auction on eBay through a component-based integration

- A suite of portals and composite applications that improved efficiency and decision support at a high-tech manufacturer

- An advanced portal implementation at an international chemicals firm that increased support for cross-functional and cross-divisional collaboration

Enterprise Services Architecture is not something that can be implemented only after years of preparation; it can actually be part of each project of an IT department.

Supply Chain Automation and an International Footwear Company

International manufacturing is a fiendishly complex enterprise at every layer. A typical shoe may pass through seven or eight factories and processing centers in five or six countries. Design, demand planning, supply, plant management, customs, labor laws, shipping, and different styles of manufacturing all must be coordinated. On top of this, the market demand is volatile and products range from low-volume, high-priced shoes to high-volume, price-sensitive shoes.

This example describes how an international footwear company tamed that complexity through use of a supply chain automation system based on Enterprise Services Architecture (see Figure 2-1). The company has completely outsourced the physical manufacturing of all of its shoes, but monitors absolutely everything about the suppliers, manufacturers, and shipping companies so that the firm can work in close cooperation with each partner and also reap the benefits of the information that is collected about each process.

The system starts with a network of 70 nodes spread across 15 different firms. At each node, information is collected via component-based integration with plant and inventory equipment, traditional EAI integration, web services, and manual data entry where needed.

On top of this information collection are several different layers of systems for different purposes. Historical information about processes, costs, sales data, and supplier and manufacturer performance is used in a composite application for demand planning. These estimates of when and how many shoes need to be produced are used to coordinate purchase and assembly of supplies, all of which is monitored by the supply chain system.

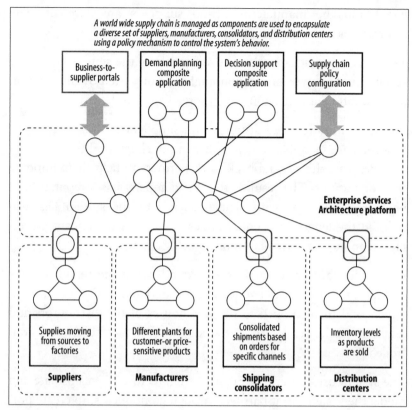

Figure 2-1. Supply chain automation

The design information that shows exactly how each shoe is put together is shared with the tier 1 manufacturers who assemble the shoes and with the tier 2, 3, and 4 manufacturers who create various component parts. All of these firms collaborate with the home office of the shoemaker through business-to-supplier portals.

The production process monitors each component part and the dependencies down the supply chain. The configuration of the supply chain is controlled by a process abstraction. The structure of the dependencies of the chain are controlled by setting policies, not by writing code. This structure allows the make-to-order low-volume processes to be implemented by the same system that manages the make-to-stock high-volume shoes, even though the processes are different and the manufacturers and suppliers are different. The abstractions make them look the same to the system.

This system provides a complete awareness of the state of the entire supply chain. A typical decision might be supported by information from 20 different collection points spread around the world.

The system has reduced disputes with suppliers and manufacturers. Problems are identified much earlier in the chain, and the company provides a wealth of data back to its partners to help them improve their operations. The result is that the company has a reputation of being easy to work with. The efficiency of the system has also reduced the length of product cycles, which is a significant advantage in an industry where fashions quickly change.

Of course, the supply chain then extends from the manufacturers and monitors the shoes as they are consolidated into the right containers and then shipped to the warehouses of the distributors and retailers. Each step of this processes is also monitored and controlled.

The system uses Enterprise Services Architecture to encapsulate and model the systems at it partners through components, to create portals to enhance collaboration with suppliers, to create composite applications for demand planning and decision support, and to control processes through a modeling environment expressed as policies for each part of the supply chain. All of the external data funnels into a suite of enterprise applications like ERP, CRM, product data management, legal and compliance systems, and document management systems, each of which is encapsulated by components that allow information to be routed in and out.

As one of the senior architects of the system put it, "The system allows us to treat process as a continuum that flows effortlessly across enterprise boundaries, which are, from an efficiency and optimization perspective, artificial barriers."

Manufacturing Plant Maintenance

Plant maintenance is the process of making sure all of the equipment at a manufacturing plant is efficient, safe, and running in optimal condition. Outages can be extremely costly. If a crucial piece of equipment fails, an entire assembly line or other manufacturing process may come to a halt. It is not uncommon for such shutdowns to cost hundreds of thousands of dollars an hour.

The typical process for maintaining plant equipment is primarily reactive. Of course, there is a typical maintenance schedule, but when something fails, a two-stage process begins. First, technicians travel to diagnose the problem and determine what parts are needed to fix the problem. Once the parts have been located to complete the task of repairing the machine, technicians make a second trip to do the repair.

The goal of the composite application used for plant maintenance that we will describe is to reduce the number of visits required to fix a piece of equipment and to increase the amount of work done on each visit.

The process of keeping large-scale manufacturing equipment working can be quite complex. A best practices approach divides the task into five stages: daily maintenance, proactive maintenance, organizational excellence, engineered reliability, and operational excellence, with 23 different key areas spread among these stages.

The traditional goals of plant maintenance are to achieve reliability and production at minimum cost, to protect the value and extend the life of existing equipment to avoid costly replacement for as long as possible, to optimize productivity of the machines, and to comply with stricter safety and environmental regulations. To further complicate matters, retirements and staff reductions constantly decrease the amount of informally preserved relevant knowledge.

A large producer of electricity solved this problem using a composite application aimed at improving efficiency, knowledge capture about the workings of plant equipment, and decision support capability (see Figure 2-2). The application also automates programs for risk-assessment and performance improvement.

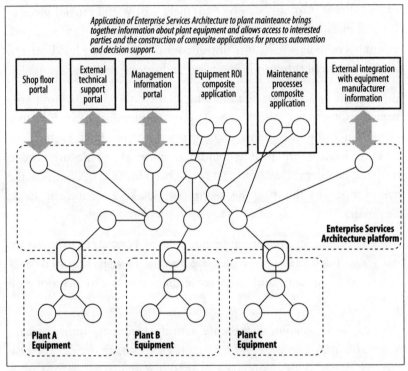

Figure 2-2. Manufacturing plant maintenance

The system is based on components that perform basic information capture on each piece of equipment. Where the equipment has real-time monitoring, that information is provided through the components. For some equipment, status data is entered on the shop floor. The result is a much more timely and accurate information flow as well as a historical record.

On top of these basic information-gathering components, several layers of applications were constructed. The first focused on providing workers on the shop floor all the data and documentation needed to make the most out of each opportunity to service the system. Technicians now routinely check the manufacturer's web site each time equipment is serviced to see if any maintenance advisories have been posted. If any are found, they are applied during the already scheduled maintenance window. When outages do occur, staff on the shop floor work with experts who have remote access to the system to determine what is wrong. Technicians can then arrive at the plant with the right parts already in hand.

Executive staff were able to construct more accurate models of the ROI for each piece of equipment because more data was available. The IT staff was able to construct a more comprehensive view of all of the information within one plant and across all plants. For example, with the new system, it is now possible to examine the performance of a piece of equipment in every location to identify problems or best practices that should be disseminated. The system also supports more advanced maintenance processes desired by management. All of this gradually increases the documented expertise about how best to run the equipment at the plant.

Collecting information into a unified repository, extending the availability of the system to the people who need it, and building additional functionality on top shows how the abstraction and componentization of Enterprise Services Architecture can make a large difference in an industrial company.

Auction Marketplace Integration

A new extension to asset management systems shows the power of Enterprise Services Architecture to transform a clunky, costly process of disposing of idle and obsolete assets into a increased revenue stream (see Figure 2-3).

Idle assets such as depreciated equipment or obsolete inventory are a fact of life. Companies have three choices when it comes to getting rid of them:

- Pay a liquidator to take the assets off the company's hands

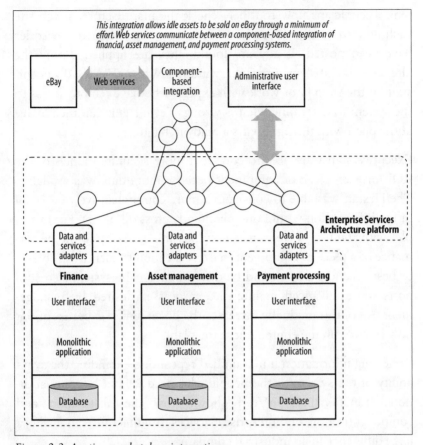

Figure 2-3. Auction marketplace integration

- Sell assets through a traditional auction firm, which usually returns about 6 to 10 cents on the dollar

- Donate the assets for a tax deduction

SAP's Asset Remarketing solution offers a fourth choice that usually returns 30 to 40 cents on the dollar through an integration between eBay and mySAP™ ERP or mySAP™ CRM. Under this solution, which is implemented through components created in SAP's Enterprise Services Architecture platform, SAP NetWeaver, the asset management module supplies a description of the assets to eBay. The articles are put up for auction through the use of web services on all sides. Once the auction takes place and a buyer has been found, the order is sent to the appropriate system for fulfillment. The asset management module helps complete the fulfillment and the financial module takes it off the books. Payment is processed through a company's existing payment mechanisms or through PayPal.

eBay is becoming an increasingly important business-to-business (B2B) channel. More than $2 billion B2B transactions took place on the site in 2002. SAP's integration allows a company to take advantage of the channel with a minimum of development through the use of a packaged integration.

Enterprise Services Architecture encapsulates the data and functionality from enterprise applications in support of a flexible, component-based integration with eBay based on web services. The flow of information back and forth is controlled through an administrative interface that allows configuration of the process rather than requiring it to be hard-coded.

Application Enablement, Simplification, and Aggregation at a High-Tech Manufacturer

A high-tech manufacturer of chips and electronic components found that Enterprise Services Architecture could be used to unlock the value of existing applications, which were underutilized and confined to a small number of expert employees. Enterprise Services Architecture expanded the applications to new users, allowed them to be used consistently and effectively, and provided a more sophisticated real-time model of the business. The implementation, shown in Figure 2-4, proceeded through three stages: empowerment and enablement, simplification, and aggregation.

Empowerment and Enablement

This high-tech firm had mature systems that provided an efficient automation of business processes. Some important interfaces were

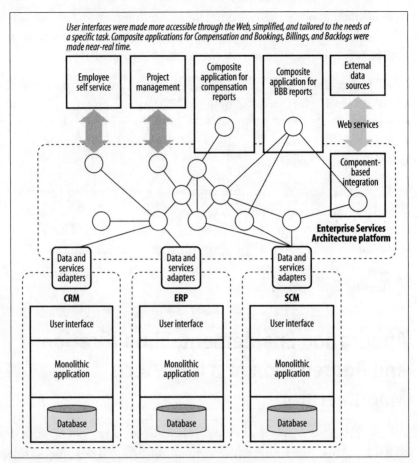

Figure 2-4. User interface enablement, simplification, and aggregation at a high-tech manufacturer

contained within client/server programs installed only on certain PCs, reducing the usage of various systems.

The first step involved using the APIs of the enterprise applications to create web-based user interfaces for such functions as expense reports, timesheets, address changes, and benefits information queries. The interfaces were tailored to a specific task and brought together just the information needed to perform that task quickly and efficiently. The improvement in accessibility and design of the user interfaces had a dramatic effect on increasing usage.

Simplification

The second step forward involved building on the accessibility of the web interfaces to create simplified user interfaces that brought together information from many different parts of the enterprise applications. The enterprise software provided interfaces similar to a NASA control room in its complexity. Everything could be managed and changed through interfaces, but they were not tailored for any one particular job. Users had to sift through this complexity to find information that was important to them, and this decreased usage. For example, a project management system that was otherwise completely functional had an interface that required traversing 14 different screens to update project status.

A set of components was built on top of the project management system and consolidated the functions of the 14 screens into 1 web-based interface. This increased the timeliness and accuracy of the information.

The benefits to the corporation were dramatic. Usage of these newly accessible applications soared. Access to employee self service applications almost tripled and reached 80 percent of the highest possible utilization. The number of failed workflow processes that expired because they sat too long waiting to be addressed by someone dropped from 20 a day to 1 or 2 a week. The number of people needed in the Human Resources call center staff dropped from seven to two full-time equivalents.

Aggregation

The third step involved aggregation of data from sources inside and outside the company. The annual compensation report created by the Human Resources department improved service and decreased costs through automation. Every year, the company created a compensation package for each employee showing the entire range of compensation including health insurance, pension and 401k contributions, and other benefits. This process took a couple of months of work every year. This system was replaced with a real-time view of all this information based on aggregation of the compensation information in a data warehouse. The annual project was eliminated and employees could find out the status of all of their compensation-related benefits on demand. Over 90 percent of employees used this system in the first year that it was launched.

The center of most high-tech manufacturers is a booking, billings, and backlog (BBB) report that gives an indication of the demand and production capacity of a company. This report was automated and based on a data warehouse, populated by integrations with systems inside and outside the company through components. The BBB report became much closer to a real-time snapshot and gave the CEO and the management team the information that they had always wanted to see, aggregated in the way they wanted to see it.

This fundamental approach of increasing the value of existing enterprise applications through enablement, simplification, and aggregation was repeated many times. The IT department found that the skills developed in creating these new interfaces were reused over and over just like the components that were created. The Enterprise Services Architecture tools were much easier to use than the APIs of the enterprise applications. Once components were constructed, the backlog of IT projects shrank dramatically.

Advanced Portal Implementation at an International Chemicals Manufacturer

Our final example tells the story of an innovative use of portal technology by an international manufacturer of chemicals and industrial products based in the United States. The company has been assembled over its 90-year history as a product of many mergers and has operations in several different chemical and high-technology related businesses that span the globe.

The architectural challenge for the firm is to bring together the functionality needed for a diverse set of businesses in such a way that the corporate office has clear and timely visibility into the operations of each division. The international reach of the company and the range of activities in the divisions amplify the difficulty of this task. It has operations in more than 20 countries, making chemicals and materials for everything from consumer products to industrial microelectronics.

The architectural vision for the company is a core single instance of SAP R/3, which is used to run the financial and accounting activities of all divisions, supplemented by enterprise applications for human resources, CRM, product lifecycle management, and supply chain management. The company has significant B2B integrations with industry-related exchanges through EAI technology.

An incremental implementation of Enterprise Services Architecture aims to increase ease of use and ease of access by tailoring user interfaces to provide each role in the company with the information and functionality needed to do the best possible job. To achieve this goal, the company brings together information from most of their enterprise applications and incorporates important news and data sources from outside the company.

The company has a three-pronged approach to portals. They are used to create bundles of services for managing the enterprise (employee self-service, manager self-service), aggregations of process-centric business information (called business information portals), and portals that support communities of interest. The leader of portal implementation at the company says that the portal implementations create value in several ways.

One such benefit is cross-functional collaboration. Community of interest portals bring together people with similar job functions from across the enterprise, allowing them to share information and collaborate in a many-to-many relationship that was not previously possible. An example of this is the communicator's portal used heavily in this job function at all levels of the company. Public relations executives who distribute information to people and governments near the company's plants find valuable information there and learn from those who are focused on communicating with the company's employees or with investors. The portal has kept the company's message coherent across these communication channels and resulted in significant reuse of materials.

Another important theme is aggregation of process-centric information. The company has significant international supply operations, and it found that by assembling information for forecasting product demand and for production planning, important news would arrive much faster at the right desktops, especially news from external sources that might take weeks to show up in the mainstream press, resulting in a smoother supply chain. Senior management will use a digital dashboard for the enterprise to provide a unified view of the company.

The manager and employee self-service portals have reduced the burden on central staff and provide direct access to applications that were previously so complex that they could be used only by experts.

One of the most successful aspects of the portal implementations has been the way that information from the enterprise applications has been combined with collaborative functionality. A simple team room, a central repository with a simple classification of documents, has addressed some of the negative aspects of unstructured collaboration such as email. Because documents were stored in a shared area, it unclogged everyone's inbox and created a historical archive. Documents could be found when needed, instead of having to contact the author of the presentation. The team room also made it easier to look at all of the presentations being produced by a team to build on them and to make sure that they were consistent.

The theory of this architecture is the portal as a flexible UI layer that contains and unifies the specialized systems at each division. Building on this solid base of portal technology, the company is extending ERP and divisional systems to the portals through Enterprise Services Architecture components.

These Enterprise Services allow for the creation of simple composite applications that contain a mix of structured and unstructured information. The targets for the first generation of these applications are optimization of business processes: credit memo processing, supplier management, and demand planning. These applications combine information from the portal, enterprise applications, and the data warehouse with collaborative functionality to create simple composite applications (see Figure 2-5).

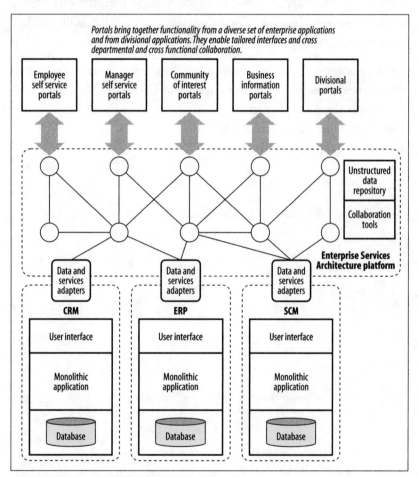

Figure 2-5. Advanced portal implementation

External communication is handled through EAI technology. The development of components for integration has started with the supply chain integration through direct connections to vendors, mostly through EAI gateways, and trading partner integration with Rosetta-Net (electronics marketplace) and Elemica (chemicals marketplace).

Patterns have already started to emerge and the company is taking advantage of common structures for portals and composite applications to prevent a proliferation of specialized code that must be maintained. The total cost of ownership of implementing Enterprise Services Architecture is reduced through using templates to reduce the maintenance burden. The templates provide flexibility in key areas but keep standards in place everywhere else.

The examples we have just examined illustrate a variety of different approaches that can be used to implement Enterprise Services Architecture. In the next chapter, we examine both sides of the business case for Enterprise Services Architecture.

3

Making the Business Case

When it comes to justifying expenditure on IT, ROI is king. There is nothing that will open up a CFO's checkbook faster than a thorough analysis that shows how spending $1 million dollars can save $10 million.

Sometimes CTOs and CIOs actually have the data to make a hard ROI case. For infrastructure projects such as data center consolidation or migration to cheaper servers, the ROI can be firmly nailed down because the beginning- and end-states are clearly defined and the costs of each can be specified accurately and in detail.

But the slam-dunk, easy-to-calculate ROI cases are the exception. For most IT projects, ROI is a reasonable hope, not a certainty. The costs are pretty clear for the first few stages, but not for those more than a year out. The benefits are frequently tangible—saving time, saving money, or eliminating waste—but the models are fuzzy. Changing a few assumptions within reasonable bounds can dramatically alter the predicted return.

Executives are not hoodwinked into approving IT projects. In the end, they share the faith of the CTO or CIO that investments in technology will pay off. Most IT projects are pursued with the idea that the company will get some hard benefits, some soft benefits, but will be better off in the end. Frequently, intangible benefits such as increasing flexibility or providing more information for decision makers are among the most important drivers. As one IT executive put it, "When you have the ROI case, use it. When you don't, call it strategic and do it anyway."

But after a decade of heady spending during the Internet boom, skepticism abounds. The faith required to hand over a large sum of money to the technology department is hard to come by.

Aggravating this hostile environment for IT spending is the difficulty of making the case for spending on architecture and platforms. The IT department has never been good at arguing for this sort of spending. The benefits are frequently intangible and hard to quantify. Email servers were not justified on an ROI basis, but few would deny that they benefit most companies.

This chapter presents the arguments on both sides of Enterprise Services Architecture that will be key to making or losing the case for improving architecture. We will review and expand on the case we made in Chapter 1. However, we will also focus on the strongest arguments against Enterprise Services Architecture. We will give Enterprise Services Architecture a rhetorical stress test and see how well it holds up.

The Case for Enterprise Services Architecture

The most persuasive arguments for Enterprise Services Architecture are specific to a particular business. Enterprise Services Architecture is most compelling when the executive team has a shared vision of a business strategy that will crush the competition and make customers joyfully send in more orders. When this vision is enabled and supported by technology built for flexibility, the comprehensive architecture we have discussed makes the most sense.

Each company must provide the vision that meets its specific set of conditions. In the following discussion, we will examine the arguments about whether fulfilling any vision with Enterprise Services Architecture is the optimal choice.

To begin, we review the case we have made so far. In Chapter 1, our analysis started with the observation that monolithic architectures are complex, inflexible, costly, change-resistant, and a creativity bottleneck. Our proposal is that focusing on our particular flavor of service-oriented architecture could change all that. The core assumptions of Enterprise Services Architecture are that:

- We will consciously design a comprehensive architecture based on our current needs and predictions about future business conditions
- We will use our current systems as a foundation
- We will create flexibility where we need it using loosely coupled components and services as the fundamental building blocks
- The resulting architecture will decrease the cost of change, which will in turn expand tactical and strategic possibilities that should enable business advantage

Such an architecture opens the way for rapid development of role-based user interfaces, composite applications, and component-based integration, which will be the enablers of a new frontier for automation. These methods of taking advantage of Enterprise Services Architecture will allow for:

- The automation of cross-functional and strategic processes that combine transactional systems, unstructured information, and collaborative functionality
- Tailored interfaces that meet the needs of new populations of users, expanding the reach of the IT infrastructure
- The extension of automation through interfaces and integrations for customers and suppliers

Benefits of this automation will include:

- Faster decision-making
- The ability to take action to correct problems or adjust processes by reaching back into enterprise applications through components

- An increase in instrumentation of the business with many more metrics about the details of business processes

- Cheaper and tighter integrations with suppliers and customers

- Extension of the functionality of existing systems to new user groups

- Support for smaller market niches

The flexibility of Enterprise Services Architecture will be required in the future because of growing customer power, increased direct access to corporate systems, and more competition.

Furthering the Case

Arguing for more flexibility and better architecture is like coming out in favor of Mom and apple pie. But given the impact of intangibles in making weighty decisions about IT spending, we believe that no argument is too small to be considered.

In this section, we consider additional arguments in favor of Enterprise Services Architecture. While the enthusiasm we display may give the impression that we are in favor of flexibility for its own sake, we are not. In Chapter 6, we examine different ways to determine how much flexibility is needed at a company.

In arguing for the ascendance of service-oriented architectures (SOAs) such as Enterprise Services Architecture, we are in good company:

- John Hagel, a former McKinsey consultant, recently authored *Out of the Box* (Harvard Business School Press), a book in support of service-oriented architecture.

- Yefim Natis, Vice President and Distinguished Analyst at Gartner, has also written numerous reports in favor of adopting SOA in a variety of circumstances.

- Vinod Khosla, a venture capitalist at Kleiner, Perkins, Caufield, & Byers, has been advocating the idea of a real-time enterprise based on service-oriented architecture for several years.

- Andy Mulholland, CTO of Cap Gemini Ernst & Young, pro-
  motes service-based architecture as the foundation of his firm's
  concept of the Adaptive Enterprise. (He expands on the relationship of this concept to Enterprise Services Architecture in the
  Afterword to this book.)

To extend our case for service-oriented architecture in general and
Enterprise Services Architecture in particular, we will review what
these gentlemen have to say and provide a few additional arguments.

A Consultant's View

The box John Hagel refers to in *Out of the Box* is a collection of limitations. He argues that companies increasingly find themselves
trapped in assumptions and beliefs that restrict choice and the ability to compete. The boxes he refers to are financial pressures, the
limitations of the current IT infrastructure, the narrow focus within
the confines of the enterprise, and mental models that favor a mech-
anistic vision of a micromanaged enterprise rather than a wider and
deeper view of processes that cross company boundaries and unlock
the value of resources outside the company.

Hagel sees web services technology and distributed services architecture, which he calls web services architecture, as a way to increase
freedom and to help escape these boxes. In the near term, Hagel predicts companies will deploy web services architecture to achieve
operational efficiencies and worries that these smaller victories will
obscure the larger potential benefits.

The ultimate prize for Hagel is to employ the flexibility and collaboration enabled by this new architecture to create substantial growth
by expanding the view of the enterprise and finding ways to mobi-
lize and leverage assets outside of a company. To achieve the full
benefit, managers will have to retool their thinking about how to
organize a business and plan and execute strategy. He outlines a
path forward for this evolution through stages of finding near-term
profitability, creating focus, and accelerating growth. The entire the-

ory rests on the foundation of web services architecture making existing systems gradually more flexible.

An Analyst's View

Yefim Natis predicts that by 2008, it is highly likely that service-oriented architecture will be a "prevailing software engineering practice, ending the 40-year domination of monolithic software architecture." In his series of research reports on service-oriented architecture, Natis lucidly describes the moving parts and portrays service-oriented architecture as "fundamentally, a flow and a relationship of service interfaces." In this model, the work done by the application takes place through a series of invocations of services, each of which has an interface designed for a particular part of the work. Service interface is at the center of application design. For this reason, Natis thinks that "interface-oriented architecture" might be a more accurate name for service-oriented architecture.

Design of effective service interfaces can be difficult. Applications with limited scope and shelf life that are not intended for reuse or ongoing extension will gain little benefit from investment in SOA, and thus are not good candidates for this approach, Natis says. Clarity of design, opportunity for incremental deployment and change, component reuse, and simplified process composition are the key benefits of service-oriented architecture.

Natis notes that service-oriented architecture is typically used in a request/reply manner, each service subordinate to its requestor. He contrasts service-oriented architecture with event-driven architecture in which each process node in the architecture performs work autonomously, with no dependence or knowledge of the rest of the system. Event-driven architecture is superior for automating back-end business processes and inter-application processes, including B2B. In contrast, service-oriented architecture is best suited for composite and multi-channel request/reply applications.

Natis believes that the ultimate architectural pattern for the modern agile enterprise is a hybrid that is service-oriented and event-driven.

Natis's analysis is packed with caution against thinking of service-oriented architecture as a solution to all problems. He points out that design and development in this architecture are a significant undertaking and that development tools are just beginning to become available. He also takes a skeptical view of web services as a panacea and predicts that web services will not be a magic bullet that will create ubiquitous interoperability. Web services interfaces will gradually be provided by application vendors, but interoperability across vendors will remain technically challenging and functionally limited for the next several years. He points out that most projects will require significant development of integration layers to translate between different data models, protocols, and interface formats, despite the growing use of Web services standards.

Despite the limitations, Natis predicts that "over time, lack of SOA-based applications and skills will become a dangerous competitive disadvantage for most enterprises." He recommends that companies invest today in understanding—through research and experience—the benefits, risks, and best practices of service-oriented architecture.

A Venture Capitalist's View

Vinod Khosla's view is that companies should optimize their architecture for "evolvability." Firms should attempt to sustain a process of continuous migration of all of their systems. He proposes four rules for IT transformation that call on companies to plan on being wrong, but to design their architectures to allow them to be optimized at all levels toward a better structure in a series of small steps involving three- to six-month project cycles. Ideally, the architecture should extend deep into the operations of all business partners.

As part of this implementation, the architecture is split into five layers:

- A delivery layer that provides the user interface or the integration between applications
- A layer of composite applications and services in which services from underlying enterprise applications are assembled into useful components

- A web services layer that supports the composite applications
- An information layer that creates a unified model of data from heterogeneous sources
- A layer of existing enterprise applications

Such an architecture creates an environment for mass customization. Just as end users configure spreadsheets to their own specific purposes, applications should be configurable to allow processes and interfaces to be tuned by the end user to the task at hand. At every level, business analysts, developers, and information modelers should be empowered to change and optimize applications. The goal should be to move as much configuration as possible to the least skilled area.

With the right separation of layers and encapsulation, each sort of technology can evolve at its own pace. "Monolithic applications are like the Russian economy under communism. Everything is planned and is supposed to work," Khosla says. "Service-oriented architectures are like democracy. Lots of small pieces that move independently provide a lot more flexibility. Change should be a process, not an event."

A Systems Integrator's View

In the Afterword, Andy Mulholland presents his view of the Adaptive Enterprise, which requires Adaptive IT. His argument contrasts the old world, where the rate of change was low and most likely under the control of the enterprise, with the new world, in which volatility is high and the ability to rapidly adapt to new conditions can create massive benefits. We refer the reader to the Afterword for the details, but his conclusion is that Enterprise Services Architecture can play a key role in gaining the flexibility needed to win in current business conditions.

A common theme runs through the arguments of these service-oriented architecture proponents: an increasing amount of flexibility is going to be required, and it must be achieved through architecture.

Each of these people has an agenda: Hagel sells consulting services, Netis sells research and advice, Khosla has a company called Asera that fits into this theory, and Mulholland sells integration projects. But it is telling, and perhaps compelling, that each of them is to some extent staking his credibility on promoting service-oriented architecture.

Additional Arguments for Enterprise Services Architecture

To augment the force of these arguments, this section describes several related points that can be made in favor of service-oriented architectures such as Enterprise Services Architecture.

Easier integration

The cost of integration is a significant barrier to innovation because the benefit of the integration must exceed the cost of implementation. When the only path is using APIs that expose the complexity of a monolithic application, the cost of integration and maintenance is high, which reduces the number of viable integration opportunities.

The cost of implementing and maintaining integrations drops dramatically in an architecture in which the core data and functionality of enterprise applications has been exposed as services. This arrangement allows more integrations to be viable and their scope to be broader, providing more functionality. It also lowers the bar for supporting outsourcing opportunities that require some sort of integrated connection to the provider.

Structural benefits

The way that Enterprise Services Architecture increases abstraction has benefits beyond flexibility. If a company's systems are encapsulated in a well-organized set of components, it may increase the value of divisions that may be sold off since the cost of separating them from the company's infrastructure is reduced. It is also possible to accelerate the retirement of systems, because the abstraction reduces the trauma of changing underlying systems that are not visible to the user. Larger changes that reduce the number of systems or dramatically alter the business process are the path to significant benefits. Optimization to get three to four percent more efficiency is no longer compelling. Changing processes or retiring systems to get 30 to 40 percent savings gets much more attention.

Unified customer view

In general, customer information is almost always among the data exposed through services for use by other components. Data services that allow for reading and writing customer information provide a powerful foundation for a virtual or replicated master repository of customer data. Such a unified view of the customer fosters a comprehensive understanding of all relationships with customers and makes it available to applications that manage touchpoints with the user. Applications can then react to this information and provide offers or additional services to customers that are tuned to the customer based on all available information.

Unlocking creativity

Behavioral research shows that if a pigeon is rewarded one out of three times for pecking a lever, it will continue the behavior. The antithesis is also true, as we see in IT departments. People who are always told no when they have an idea eventually stop trying. Perhaps the most stifling effect of an inflexible IT infrastructure is the reduction in creativity.

When an architectural plan takes years to implement, and everything else must go to the bottom of the list, no suggestions are welcome. Shortening a long road map can dramatically increase the benefit of any architectural changes by bringing it online sooner and encouraging creativity for further innovation.

With these rosy thoughts in mind, we now examine the arguments against Enterprise Services Architecture.

The Case Against Enterprise Services Architecture

In this section we summon the voice of the naysayer, the skeptic, the person who looks at the world as a festering mass of problems that only gets worse. To such a person, the suggestion of any change, any potential improvement, is a step in the wrong direction. We will use this character to examine the arguments that are likely to be used against proposals for improved architecture. If Enterprise Services Architecture has a hope, it will have to withstand such attacks.

Endless Design and Requirements Cycles

"Sure, Enterprise Services Architecture is a great idea," the skeptics will say. "But the design process will never end. There are Dilbert cartoons aplenty about endless requirements cycles. These cycles go on and on, not because of the quality of the ideas being considered, but because of the lack of political will and clarity of vision needed to make decisions about trade-offs. And even if this will is found, the design problem presented by Enterprise Services Architecture is too large to be managed by even the most well-run organizations."

This is one of the most powerful arguments against not only Enterprise Services Architecture but really any large change that requires planning and design. Requirements cycles generally lack a good understanding of project goals, which would allow priorities to be established and provide a basis for making trade-offs. Enterprise Services Architecture tries to combat an endless loop of design and requirements in two ways. First, Enterprise Services Architecture starts with the humbling idea that all designs are wrong and the only way to find out how wrong is to implement them and use them. With a complete view from the battlefield, the design can then be adjusted incrementally. Second, under Enterprise Services Architecture, the amount of flexibility is guided not by the theoretical limit, but by providing just enough flexibility to enable practical business benefits.

Scarce Design Skills

"We don't have the skills to create a design the way that Enterprise Services Architecture requires," the skeptics will say. "Don't kid yourself: design and modeling are advanced skills and just because we want to create a good design does not mean we can."

It is true that design is difficult and requires skill. Generally, the more seasoned the designer or architect, the better the design. This objection actually springs from a mature attitude that it is unreasonable to expect an instant design that solves the company's problems. But it is possible to get help from consultants and, given the scarcity of design talent, acquiring the skills could provide a competitive advantage to a company. This difficulty is one reason that analysts like Netis recommend an early start.

An Operations Nightmare

"Enterprise Services Architecture is an operations nightmare," the skeptics will say. "Now, in addition to supporting our enterprise applications to an acceptable level, we will be adding a platform to support components that will be loosely coupled and will be connected in complex ways. In addition, each component will depend on others and we will have to monitor and manage the service level for each of them. How are we going to keep track of all this? Given all of these dependencies, the weakest and slowest component could bring the others to a screeching halt. This is too much to handle for even the best operations staff."

Increased complexity of operations, like design, is another cost of the flexibility of the Enterprise Services Architecture. If a company is going to offer services, each one needs a service level. A typical company manages the service level of 10 or 20 key enterprise applications. In a fully implemented Enterprise Services Architecture, 40 or 50 components and associated services may be added to this mix. This objection points out that it is not wise to assume that this will be easy. Companies should plan for this learning curve. It will be possible to meet this challenge. Vendors and standards-setters are aware that operational aspects of service-oriented architecture must be addressed for adoption to occur. In any event, this learning will be forced on companies by business partners seeking integration. Which suppliers will do better when a powerful partner like Wal-Mart insists on tighter integration? Those with sophisticated operational skills, or those who pretend that a more complex world will never arrive?

Flexibility and Interoperability Won't Be Delivered

"Vendors will never live up to their promises and deliver the flexibility and interoperability promised by service-oriented architectures," the skeptics will say. "We all know we can't believe the vision. If we rush to implement this, we will be left holding a messy and expensive bag of technology that at best almost works."

Any vision from the vendor community should be taken with a large grain of salt, especially grand ones like Enterprise Services Architecture. Vendors really have no choice but to move in the direction of service-oriented architecture. We will examine why in detail in Chapter 8. Vendors must bring down the cost of integration and must also offer more targeted products for specific functions and vertical markets in order to make customers happy and keep selling software. Service-oriented architecture is the only way to make this work. Interoperability across vendors is another story. Just because applications are accessible through services doesn't mean that services from one vendor will seamlessly talk to another. Netis points out that some sort of integration and translation will likely be required in many cases.

But the real question is not whether to buy into the wholesale vision of the vendors or not. The most important question is whether Enterprise Services Architecture and the flexibility it can bring will help your business succeed. If you are in a position where increasing amounts of flexibility will not be required or if you have another way of getting there, Enterprise Services Architecture doesn't make sense.

Development and Runtime Tools Unavailable

"The development and runtime tools don't exist yet, and they won't be ready for a couple of years," the skeptics will say. "Why struggle with version 1.0 of all of this stuff when it will actually work if I wait a bit?"

Some of the development environments for web services and other key technologies are in early versions and will clearly be better in the future. But much of the work of preparing for Enterprise Services Architecture involves understanding and analyzing core business processes, data, and existing systems. Such an understanding provides the foundation for a good design. The key question is not whether the tools will work but what should be done with them.

Standards Still Soft

"Web services and related standards are still a toy," the skeptics will say. "Security and transactions have not been nailed down and efforts to create business process modeling languages are still in their early stages. The hype is far ahead of the reality. It is best to wait until reality catches up."

Standards will be more mature and comprehensive in the future. The question again is not whether the current environment supporting Enterprise Services Architecture is perfect, but rather whether there will be a benefit to gaining the flexibility it offers. Much can be done with the current state of the technology and standards.

Why Rush? Wait and See

"With all due respect to the glorious vision of Enterprise Services Architecture, there are too many things to learn and too many gaps in the technology to justify even experimentation at this time," the skeptics will say. "Why not let others suffer and learn? Let the standards mature. Let the vendors get better at this. In three or four years we can do it much cheaper and easier."

Rushing into anything is seldom a good idea. Learning from the experience of others is also a wise policy. This objection can only be answered in the context of a specific business. How quickly do things change in your industry? How stable are business conditions? Will competitors gain an advantage from increased flexibility? Will business partners force increased automation through the supply chain? As Vinod Khosla points out, change should be a process, not an event. If we look at some of the winning companies in today's marketplace, such as Cisco, Dell, and Amazon.com, we see engines to manage change. The decision of how to build such an engine is up to each individual company. The marketplace will force most companies to take up this task.

With the arguments for and against Enterprise Services Architecture on the table, we will now take a closer look at the moving parts of the architecture.

4

Anatomy

One fundamental process is the primary function of every business. Draw a circle around the whole company and label it "Make Money." Inside that circle are all the processes and supporting systems that are used to run the business. If you had to break that "Make Money" circle into smaller chunks, what would they look like? How big should they be? How should they be connected? Answering all of these questions in a way that increases the flexibility, efficiency, and strategic choices for a company is the fundamental quest of Enterprise Services Architecture.

Enterprise Services Architecture is both a process and an end-state. As a process, it describes how to break the "Make Money" circle into the right constituent parts and determine what each part should do. As an end-state, it describes all the features that would make the infrastructure meet the highest standard of flexibility and configurability while maximizing the use of existing resources.

The process begins with an understanding of a business and its systems and moves through stages of understanding how and where to improve parts of the system to bring them closer to the Enterprise Services Architecture end-state in order to maximize business value.

In this chapter we dissect the end-state of Enterprise Services Architecture, the ideal shape for a company's systems, which can be compared to an atom or a molecule. The stable parts of the system are at the center, like protons or neutrons that are bound by a strong nuclear force. The volatile parts of the system are the equivalent of

fast-moving electrons. Enterprise Services Architecture seeks to identify the different categories in a company's complex of systems and
then understand how all the parts relate to each other. Our analysis
of the Enterprise Services Architecture end-state seeks to discover
patterns to the structure of these elemental parts that can make systems more useful.

To tell this story, we begin by reviewing our take on the appropriate
process for designing and implementing Enterprise Services Architecture. We then categorize systems according to the amount of flexibility they might need and present the idea of compliance levels to
provide a clear scale for flexibility. As we saw in the examples in
Chapter 2, there are many different ways to apply Enterprise Services Architecture. The Enterprise Services Architecture compliance
levels allow us to speak precisely about how we want to change a
system.

With all that in mind, we will then examine the detailed structure of
how the components and services will be applied to create business
value.

Enterprise Services Architecture differs from concepts like service-
oriented architecture in two important ways. First, business concerns are always fundamental for Enterprise Services Architecture.
Enterprise Services Architecture is not a goal to be achieved for its
own sake or a methodology to be applied everywhere without concern for costs or results. For many enterprise applications, it may be
appropriate to stop short of full Enterprise Services Architecture
compliance. Second, Enterprise Services Architecture assumes the
starting point is an existing base of enterprise applications, platform
component systems, and customized legacy applications. Enterprise
Services Architecture creates a better architecture not by tossing
everything onto the junk pile but by building components on top of
the existing base. Incremental progress is a basic Enterprise Services
Architecture value.

Enterprise Services Architecture as a Process

The Enterprise Services Architecture process includes four stages:

Research
> Understanding existing systems and how they support a business

Forecasting
> Determining where to apply Enterprise Services Architecture by predicting areas of the business that are likely to change and require agility

Design
> Designing the architecture, objects, services, and components that sit on top of existing systems and support the need for flexibility, optimization of processes, or new supplier relationships

Implementation
> Building the new architecture in a series of small steps, each of which brings the architecture closer to the desired level of compliance

The research stage is designed to bring a company into the first level of Enterprise Services Architecture compliance in which the contribution of each system is understood in detail. This stage helps inventory the basic parts available to the architect for improving the architecture. At this stage, the architect identifies the basic data objects, services, and processes that occur inside a business, making a map that describes how existing systems automate the most important processes.

The forecasting stage involves looking outside of IT to the customer base, marketplace, and economic and regulatory environment to discover the elemental forces that are likely to affect the business. In this stage, the company acts like a military general, analyzing the current position of the battlefield, planning future missions, anticipating what the opponent might do, and forecasting changing conditions.

The design stage is perhaps the most challenging. The company acts like a manufacturer and must place bets based on the forecast. The bets take the form of investment in componentizing parts of applications, just like an auto company designs the subsystems for its cars. As we will see later in our discussion of the levels of compliance, the work done to increase compliance can take many forms. It may mean dramatic changes for an enterprise application or no changes at all. The design stage is where the practical limits of available resources must be balanced against the cost of improving the architecture and the potential benefits that might accrue. Design must take into account incremental implementation just as the design of automobile components is informed by how the components are assembled.

The implementation stage selects a certain set of architectural improvements to be realized. The challenge of this phase is to take meaningful steps forward in short time frames so that progress can be demonstrated and assumptions in the forecast and design can be validated.

In Chapter 6, we discuss a host of issues related to these stages such as how detailed a description one needs of each system, how to determine where flexibility might be needed, and how to decide between creating a few large components or many smaller ones.

Enterprise Services Architecture as an End-State

The goal of the Enterprise Services Architecture end-state is to enable IT departments to answer "yes" more frequently when asked to support a new business process, automate a supplier relationship, or create a new interface to interact directly with customers. Using Enterprise Services Architecture, changes are both affordable and streamlined. An affirmative answer is possible not because absolutely everything has been made flexible but because needs have been anticipated and the right components are waiting to be configured.

The optimal Enterprise Services Architecture end-state will be different at each company because its existing systems, customers, marketplace, and forecasts are all likely to be different. But general features of the Enterprise Services Architecture end-state will be the same at each company. The Enterprise Services Architecture end-state includes these features:

Key data elements
Key data elements from all systems are available for use by composite applications.

Key services
Key services from each system have been identified and are available for composite applications.

Targeted flexibility
Flexibility in the behavior of applications that are fundamental to creating business value and are also likely to change is supported through loosely coupled components.

Common ecosystem
A common ecosystem for objects, services, and components allows components that are constructed from a heterogeneous collection of underlying enterprise applications to work together.

Modeling based on metadata
The structure and behavior of the system is controlled through modeling based on metadata in areas requiring long-term flexibility and rapid response to change.

Process modeling, not programming
The business processes and orchestration of components of the system are controlled through a process modeling environment that allows configuration of processes rather than implementation in programming languages such as Java.

Stable systems support
Stable business areas are supported with stable systems at the lowest possible cost.

Minimizing dependencies

Dependencies between systems are identified, minimized, and, where necessary, implemented in a loosely coupled fashion.

These characteristics translate into an architecture that looks like Figure 4-1.

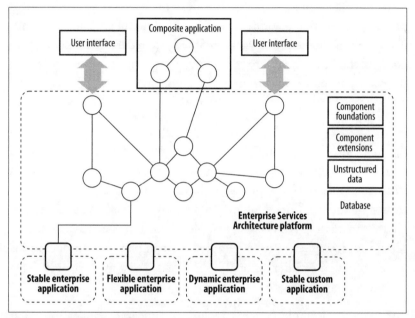

Figure 4-1. Targeted Flexibility in Enterprise Services Architecture

Enterprise Services Architecture's Impact on Various Types of Systems

The Enterprise Services Architecture end-state includes three categories of systems: stable, flexible, and dynamic.* One important technique of system construction and configuration is applied where needed: modeling based on metadata. Figure 4-1 identifies the differ-

---

* External is another system category, but such systems are outside of the boundaries and control of the enterprise. These systems and services are provided as-is and cannot be changed in any predictable way by the architects implementing Enterprise Services Architecture.

ent sorts of systems as well as the elements required for modeling. They are further defined in the following sections.

Stable systems

Stable systems are enterprise applications or legacy systems that are well-suited to solving a stable business problem. A stable business problem is one that a company believes will not change in any significant way in the next five years. Stable systems are generally mature enough that they adapt to changing needs through configuration, that is, by using settings that allow the behavior of the system to be adjusted in anticipated ways. A stable system should not require development work to continue to do its job.

Frequently, a one-to-one mapping exists between a stable system and an enterprise application or customized legacy application because stable business problems have generally received attention from software vendors. Stable systems may be available as a service. Payroll processing is a classic example. It has long been available as a service and, while it can be complex for companies with operations across regional or international boundaries, the way payroll systems change is well understood.

Other sorts of stable systems include mainframe applications that have been running for 30 years, or a part of an enterprise application. For a part of an enterprise application to be declared a stable system, it must be distinguishable from the parts of the enterprise application that may have to change. Any dependencies between the unstable and stable parts have to be understood so that the claim of stability is justifiable. For example, in an industry undergoing a revolution in manufacturing techniques, taking an order may be stable, but making the product may not be.

Typically, stable systems do not provide a competitive advantage. They often provide functionality that is on the verge of becoming a commodity. However, it is possible to imagine a stable system with significant strategic value. A proprietary system that performs a unique function that is unlikely to change may be a stable system that provides competitive advantage.

Stable systems are highly likely to be the master repository for much of the important data about a company's operations. For this reason, stable systems are likely to comply with at least Enterprise Services Architecture level 2, which exposes the data in the system in a way that can be used by composite applications and other enterprise applications. (Details about each of the Enterprise Services Architecture levels are provided later in this chapter.)

Legacy applications are perfect examples of stable systems and also illustrate why systems are stable. At some point in their career, most users and developers have encountered an anachronistic system. All of a sudden one feels the jolt of time travel as a user interface out of the mid-1980s appears on the screen.

Such systems stay around for many reasons, such as the cost of replacing the system or the unavailability of source code. The company may lack the expertise to recreate the system. While these reasons may partially explain the long shelf life of certain applications, another important reason presents itself: such applications remain because the business problem they were meant to solve is stable.

Consider this argument. If the business problem were not stable, the application would have had to be retired long ago because generally such applications are unchangeable. The cost of recreating applications has generally dropped as development tools and operating systems have become more powerful. If the application were not providing business value, it would have been shut down because of high maintenance costs. IT departments generally try to reduce the number of applications as a matter of efficiency and cost savings. In a well-run IT shop, the most plausible explanation for the long shelf life of certain systems is that the business problem they address has not changed much.

Stable systems relate to the end-state of Enterprise Services Architecture as follows: the amount of flexibility required in any part of the Enterprise Services Architecture end-state should be inversely related to the stability of the business problem being solved.

Flexible systems

Flexible systems are likely to change in the next two years in a way that may require development. Such systems also offer valuable services for composite applications or for other enterprise applications.

The likelihood of change means that an architect should seek to identify what is important about the application and present an abstraction of the functionality to other programs as a service. If a number of related services and data objects are provided by the flexible system, a component comprised of a number of related objects and services should be provided.

The ideal design of services or components for a flexible system attempts to anticipate where change will occur. It would be a mistake, for example, to design a widely used service with elements that are frequently subject to change. It would reduce the cost of change in the future if the services were designed so the most widely used ones would be the most stable. We discuss many more issues related to the design of services in the later sections on Enterprise Services Architecture levels 3 and 4.

Flexible systems tend to be more strategic and proprietary. If they are based on enterprise applications, they typically involve some special use of the data or some additional functionality that provides unique value to the business. An architecture typically has fewer flexible systems than stable systems. Flexible systems offer the sort of services defined in Enterprise Services Architecture level 3 at a minimum and probably will have parts that are components as defined in level 4.

Dynamic systems

Dynamic systems are expected to change frequently in significant ways. Dynamic systems support real-time decision making and business process optimization. Dynamic systems are focused on assembling information from a wide variety of sources, analyzing it, and then taking action on it. In this respect they frequently cross the boundaries between automation and collaboration.

Dynamic systems are like a model of the enterprise with different components representing different entities. The processes and analytics that are related to these components must change as fast as business conditions change to remain relevant. Dynamic systems must have the capability to keep up. New problems, processes, or analytics may mean that new components are constructed to represent them. Components that are no longer relevant may fall by the wayside. A dynamic system is like the short list of what is important to the enterprise.

Dynamic systems represent a new kind of application that has only been made possible by the recent build-out of enterprise applications and infrastructure. In the past few years, the amount of information collected about a business and its processes has grown dramatically with the implementation of each new application. Dynamic systems were created out of these parts and as such are frequently composite applications. Generally, they replace or automate the sort of ad hoc analysis done in the flexible world of the spreadsheet.

Because dynamic systems must keep pace with changing environments, they generally comply with Enterprise Services Architecture level 4, meaning they are constructed from components, and Enterprise Services Architecture level 5, meaning that the processes of the system are configurable.

The number of dynamic systems in any architecture is likely to be small, maybe only one or two. These systems correspond to the most important value-creating processes, generally a small fraction of all of the processes that take place in a business. If the Enterprise Services Architecture platform is like a nervous system, a dynamic system is the brain.

The Role of Modeling and Metadata

Particle physicists are never satisfied with any level of abstraction. They always want to go deeper and reduce things to a more fundamental model that explains the world in a simpler way with a smaller number of parts. The strong nuclear force we spoke of earlier was at one time one of four forces, along with the weak nuclear force, elec-tromagnetism, and gravity. Physicists have reduced this to two forces, gravity and the rest, which are now understood as different incarnations of the same force.

Computer scientists are the same way. Once they have understood a problem as a set of parts or objects, they generally try to find a more fundamental abstraction that can be used to describe and build the parts at a deeper level of abstraction. The data that is used in this description of the parts is *metadata*, i.e., data about data. The way that the parts are modeled is called a *metamodel*, a model of a model. This is all much simpler than it sounds as a couple of examples will illustrate.

Universal remote controls are able to adjust settings on all models of TVs, VCRs, and DVD players. Instead of having many remote con-trols, one device for each appliance, you can control everything with one unit. Universal remote controls have the ability to communicate with any appliance through infrared or radio signals. They under-stand which signals to send to which appliance, but they don't know which appliances are at your house. To make a universal remote control work, you must tell it which device you have. Generally a remote control comes with a list of numbers that are assigned each model of TV, VCR, or DVD player. You enter the numbers of the device into the remote control so that it knows that when you press the volume button, it should send the increase volume signal that corresponds to your appliance. If you change VCRs, you don't need a new remote; you need to enter a new number to tell the remote to behave differently. The numbers that are entered into the device are metadata. A model is used to describe the way to control each device. Each of these models is described by a metamodel.

Modeling and metadata can be employed in Enterprise Services Architecture in a similar way to make changing the behavior of a sys-tem faster, less traumatic, and less costly. Changing metadata is much easier than changing source code. This technique is applicable when the objects, services, and processes are understood and a pretty good prediction can be made about how they will change. If the basic elements and their behavior are understood and change is likely, investing in modeling and metadata can be a wise decision, especially in an area that can provide significant business value.

If it is possible to describe an object, service, or process with metadata, it is generally possible to create that object, service, or process from that description. The universal remote takes the approach of building a machine that imitates the behavior of a number of different remote controls. With software, it usually works a bit differently for performance reasons. A universal object that uses a metadata description to imitate the behavior of many different objects would work but might be slow. So in many cases, source code describing a particular object is generated instead, and the object is created from the source code and runs much faster.

Using modeling and metadata may at first appear too complicated and closer to the realm of computer science than business. It is likely that software vendors will probably be the first to implement these sorts of systems. In fact, parameter files that control the configuration of enterprise application are metadata. But as the following example will show, companies have much to gain from this approach in the right situation.

Let's imagine that a company has about 20 suppliers for various parts used in manufacturing. Each supplier manufactures some parts and distributes parts from other manufacturers. The parts that are offered by each supplier change on a monthly basis and the prices change weekly. All of the suppliers provide the monthly and weekly changes in a spreadsheet. Some of the suppliers offer ways to check inventory levels online, but all are different. Some use EDI, others use a web page, and others use web services. As part of its supply chain management (SCM) system, the company needs to know how much parts will cost and how many parts are available.

This situation is ripe for the application of modeling and metadata. The first model needed is for a part. This model must be comprehensive enough to include all of the descriptions of the parts from all of the suppliers. That means that the spreadsheets that contain the part descriptions and prices must be mapped onto the common model. The mapping of the columns of the spreadsheet to the common model of the parts is contained in metadata. If a new supplier shows up, a new mapping is created.

Every week all of these spreadsheets are read into a database using the metadata mapping. The SCM system has an object that searches through the database of parts and displays those that match along with the prices. The object then has the ability to use the different online inventory query services from the suppliers. Each different type of inventory query might be handled by a subcomponent that handles the details of the communication. If a new supplier arrives with a new inventory query technique, a new subcomponent may be needed but everything else works the same.

This is a simple example of the use of metadata to support a basic mapping and of an inventory query service used to create an abstraction across a set of different services from various suppliers. If this example were in a real company, it is likely that several different things would be happening. If the company had a lot of power over its suppliers, it may ask that the spreadsheet be replaced by an XML file with a standard format. (Wal-Mart, which has a long history of demanding standardization from business partners, recently informed suppliers that all of their products must be shipped with electronic identifiers called RFIDs by 2005.) Such a requirement might make the metadata mapping unnecessary. The different methods of inventory query could be replaced by a web service, which would make the inventory query subcomponent simpler.

A natural extension of this process would be to include online purchasing of the parts. Each supplier might have a different process for purchasing based on a different set of components. If all of the services required for purchasing from suppliers were supported, the different processes for combining the services could be stored as metadata. The process metadata would describe the order in which to invoke the services for a particular supplier. If a process changed or a new supplier came with a new process based on the same service, only metadata would have to change to support the process.

Of course, the modeling and metadata approach does not make all conceivable changes inexpensive. If a new data field shows up to describe new kinds of parts or if a new type of service is used to support the purchasing process, work will have to be done. The art of modeling is to reduce the likelihood of such events and the amount of work involved in reacting to them.

It is easy to imagine the business advantages of this approach. The company using the modeling and metadata approach can support new suppliers faster, get information from them faster, and react more quickly to changes. These benefits could add up to a significant competitive advantage.

Enterprise Services Architecture Compliance Levels

The idea of Enterprise Services Architecture compliance levels was inspired by the Capability Maturity Model® (CMM), created at the Software Engineering Institute of Carnegie Mellon University. CMM, a system for evaluating and categorizing software development processes, has five levels of maturity. The first level is called "heroics," which means that you are just trying to do your best. The second through fifth levels describe higher and higher levels of sophistication that are defined by meeting certain criteria in key process areas. The progression starts with processes that are documented and then enforced. It then moves through various stages of measurement and optimization. Sarcastic developers sometimes brag to the uninitiated that their organization meets CMM level 1, without revealing that everyone does.

Enterprise Services Architecture compliance levels are much more informal than CMM levels. They exist mainly to provide a convenient set of milestones that can be used to describe a company's progress toward a better architecture. As one moves from level 1 to 5, each represents a level of abstraction with higher potential to create business value. The first level is defined as a set of questions that a company should be able to answer about its IT infrastructure. More advanced levels of abstraction are described in levels 2 through 5.

The levels imitate the natural process that most companies follow in improving their architecture. They are not formal levels like CMM, in which you cannot reach level 3 without satisfying the criteria of level 2. In Enterprise Services Architecture compliance levels, you might partially satisfy level 3 while ignoring level 2. Enterprise Services Architecture does not have to be applied comprehensively. It can be useful to carve out a portion of the infrastructure or even a part of a system for improvement using Enterprise Services Architecture principles. Enterprise Services Architecture compliance levels can apply to customized applications or enterprise applications created by software vendors. Table 4-1 summarizes the criteria for each Enterprise Services Architecture compliance level.

Table 4-1. ESA compliance levels

Level	Definition	Role of Metadata
Level 1: The Big Think	Understanding and documenting the data, objects, services, and processes that a system provides that are important to the enterprise.	None.
Level 2: Data Services	Read/write access to the objects of the system in a way that maintains the consistency of the application.	Describes the data and services that can be accessed.
Level 3: User Interface Abstraction	The ability to separate the user interface from the rest of the system so that the services can be used as components in composite user interfaces or by other systems.	Describes the services that support construction of UIs.
Level 4: Loosely Coupled Components and Services	Services and objects are grouped into components that are designed so that they can be loosely coupled.	Describes the services provided by each component.
Level 5: Process Abstraction	Processes are exposed and configurable.	Describes the services that support configurable processes.

Enterprise Services Architecture will increase abstraction during development as well as deployment. Modeling and metadata is used to support a model-driven approach to application development in which applications are created through manipulating models instead of by writing code. We will describe the potential of this new development paradigm at the end of Chapter 5.

Level 1: The Big Think—Understanding Existing Systems

The first Enterprise Services Architecture compliance level aims to develop a comprehensive understanding of how IT architecture creates value for a business. Before embarking on a program of improvement, it is important to understand where a company would benefit most from a better architecture. The Enterprise Services Architecture process starts with a research phase designed to answer all of the questions that would enable an architect to group a company's systems into the categories defined in the Enterprise Services Architecture end-state.

The first big think is focused as much on the business as on the IT infrastructure. The questions listed below and the artifacts that are created all describe various aspects of the interaction of business processes and IT systems used to automate them. The goal of Enterprise Services Architecture is not simply efficiency or flexibility but to put those attributes at the service of creating business value. To that end, the following questions are the foundation of the Enterprise Services Architecture level 1 analysis.

- What are the most important business processes?
- How many and how much of those processes are automated by enterprise applications or custom legacy applications?
- For each application, which important data objects and services may be of use to other applications?
- What data objects are most frequently shared by applications or required by the most applications?
- What is the level of Enterprise Services Architecture compliance for each application?
- What is the current backlog of IT requests?

- What are the criteria for prioritizing these requests?
- What is the current understanding of which processes and systems are likely to change over the next five years?
- Which business processes and corresponding applications are stable? Flexible? Dynamic?

As part of this analysis it is likely that the following artifacts will be created.

- A description of the business processes most important to value creation
- A description of the data required by the important processes
- A description of the services required by the important processes
- A description of all of the key applications of an enterprise, including what data objects and services they provide and what processes they support
- A description of the dependencies or integrations between key applications
- A description of the dependencies on external services and applications

It is important to put limits on such a process. It could easily take a year or more to do an exhaustive job of collecting such information and that would be a mistake. The big think should not mean a big delay. The right approach is to plan a comprehensive analysis and stage it so that incremental projects can be undertaken while the analysis continues. These projects will provide more information and will reveal important differences of opinion about which processes are most important. In fact, the big think may reveal how little the business and technology sides of a company understand each other. The answer CEOs and CIOs provide to the question of which processes are most important to a business varies widely in detail and specificity, both within a company and across different companies.

Another theme that runs through these questions is the notion that business process should be the guiding principle. The goal of these questions is not to create an exhaustive catalog of data objects and potential services but to identify those that are related to the important processes of a business. This approach provides motivation and focus for the research. It also compares data objects and services and helps determine which to address first. The one involved in the most value-creating processes is the most important one.

It would be unwise to make the first step in an Enterprise Services Architecture improvement program too broad. The level of detail should be guided by the likely scope of the improvement project. It is perfectly justifiable to focus on a smaller portion of a company's infrastructure so the entire Enterprise Services Architecture process can quickly be executed and produce some tangible results. The Enterprise Services Architecture process will be most successful if it is tailored to the needs of a specific organization and this can only happen properly through practice.

Level 2: Data Services

Enterprise Services Architecture level 2 and higher describe particular behavior of enterprise applications. These levels can be applied to technology from vendors or to custom applications. Data services allow read and write data access to other applications.

Most applications provide multiple ways to access data. The user interface is the most common, followed by application programming interfaces (APIs) that allow developers to write programs that read and write the data. Other methods similar to APIs include XML-based interfaces, EAI technology, or web services.

Data services provide an abstraction to make data access easier for other applications. Such services allow data to be read and written from an application according to the following criteria:

- The service encapsulates and manages complex data structures within the application in order to provide a simplified view of the data.

- The service supports a simple query function to find records stored in the application.

- The service checks the data for valid values and relationships.

- The service guarantees consistency of the application. The service does not allow data to be written to the application in a way that causes incorrect or inconsistent behavior.

- The service is atomic. Each request is complete in itself with no dependence on previous or future requests.

- The service is described using metadata.

The ideal implementation creates a service that replaces many instances of hard-coded integration that were implemented using APIs. Our claim is not that APIs won't get the job done. APIs are designed to provide access to data. But to use an API properly, without unintended side effects, one must understand the structure of the database and the way that the application responds to changes in the database. This is somewhat like raising the hood of a car and fiddling with the engine. To make a small adjustment, you might have to know quite a bit. Without a comprehensive understanding it is possible, for example, to write a record to a table, but fail to create records in other tables that may be required. When the application finds these records missing, errors may occur.

Of course, APIs themselves were written to encapsulate the knowledge and protect programmers from making mistakes. APIs are designed to provide some level of abstraction so a programmer does not have to read and write directly from the database. But the need to allow wide-ranging flexibility frequently makes the APIs quite complex and potentially dangerous. The designers of APIs also don't really know what level of information is required by the processes of a particular business.

Finding the right level is never easy. The design problem that the Enterprise Services Architecture architect faces is similar to the one faced by the API designer. Should I offer lots of services that give the user flexibility or should I create one large service that does everything? This design problem hits us again and again in many forms and no real general answer can be given other than to design the level of abstraction to meet current and anticipated needs and then learn from experience.

The definition of data services states that they should be atomic to keep things simple. The recommendation that valid values be checked is designed to anticipate the future in which business process analysts may be assembling composite applications out of services and components. In such a world, each service must reduce the burden on the developer and protect the application from bad data as much as possible.

Data services are a simple and powerful level of compliance that will find broad usage across all types of applications. Stable applications will probably find data services sufficient to fully participate in an Enterprise Services Architecture. Flexible and dynamic applications will also probably offer data services to provide simple access to data in addition to higher levels of abstraction.

As Figure 4-2 shows, data services work through adapters that enable the encapsulation and abstraction of data from existing enterprise applications.

Level 3: User Interface Abstraction

After companies have exposed all the data in their applications, they generally tailor the user interface for different groups of users. The application services of Enterprise Services Architecture level 3, UI Abstraction, are aimed at creating customized, role-based interfaces as easily as possible.

User interface abstraction separates application processing from the management of the user interface. This is not an easy task for most applications because user interface-oriented preparation of data tends to seep down into the application and application code tends to creep up. The distinctions are frequently hard to draw. For example, is computing a function of several variables for display on a page a user interface or application function? If it is a complicated for-

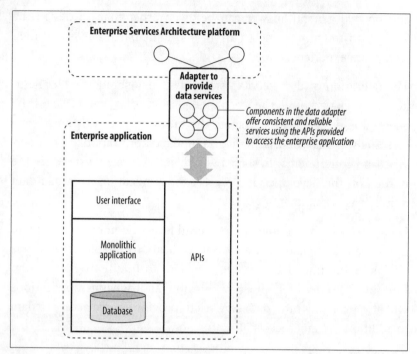

Figure 4-2. Data Services Adapter Structure

mula that will be used on many different pages, it is probably application code. If it is just formatting a percentage by multiplying a value by 100, perhaps the function should be considered as part of the user interface.

The line between the user interface and the application code can be drawn in innumerable ways. The user interface layer must be able to create pages, have some sort of unit of content that can be included in a page, and support basic elements of navigation and information display. Generally, these pages fall into certain UI patterns such as "search and display results" or "pick from a list and display detail," and so on. To work with this user interface system, the application code must provide a certain set of services needed by the user interface system that allows the application information to be delivered into units of content and participate in creating the UI patterns. Generally, it requires some way to describe the navigation, the process of moving from page to page.

Application services that support the user interface also depend on the state of the application and the previous activity of the user. An application service might behave differently if a user has not been authenticated. Certain services or activities may be available only when the application is in a specific state. For example, it might not be possible to create the order for a customer until a customer record is created.

User interface abstraction allows the architect to select services from a wide variety of applications to construct a new interface. This ability to tailor the user interface is the reason that portals have become so popular.

User interface abstraction application services meet the following criteria:

- The services are designed to participate in a user interface design and development framework.

- The services present application functionality at a level appropriate for interaction with the user interface framework.

- The services contain only application code, which is strictly separated from the user interface code.

- The services are not atomic; they may depend on application state or the actions of prior services.

- The services may be designed to participate in a user interface process control system to support navigation through areas of an application and the processes exposed by the application.

- Side effects and prerequisites of the services are well-documented.

- The services do as much as possible to protect from obvious mistakes such as bad data or invalid invocation.

- The services are described in metadata.

While the data services defined in Enterprise Services Architecture level 2 are pretty clear in their function and definition, the application services that support user interface abstraction are less concrete. These services do whatever it takes to translate the application functionality into useful chunks for a user interface. They are less precise than data services because the notion of the application is less precise than that of a database. Some application services may own data and transform it while other services may transform data handed to them. Services may also report on the status of a process. Portal systems are the most common form of user interface abstraction in the current IT environment.

UI abstraction can tailor interfaces for specific groups of users. The UI is freed from the monolith. The information that is required by a specific role in the company can be brought together to maximize value for the user. Any number of interfaces can be built for an existing set of applications. Composite applications are similar to portals but go a step further by adding new functionality of their own. Composite applications may take advantage of the application services created as part of user interface abstraction.

Most APIs provided with enterprise applications are focused on data access. The user interface of those enterprise applications is the primary gateway to the vast bulk of the application functionality. As time goes on and Enterprise Services Architecture has its effect on enterprise application vendors, it is likely that more application functionality will be exposed as services and components. We will examine this issue more deeply in Chapter 8.

Keep in mind that only a fraction of an enterprise application's functionality may need to become a service to bring substantial benefit to a large number of users. The daunting task of exposing all of the application functionality may not be needed and should not prevent architects from starting with the low-hanging fruit.

Architects will likely implement user interface abstraction in both flexible and dynamic systems that contain important information that may be of use to other groups of users (see Figure 4-3).

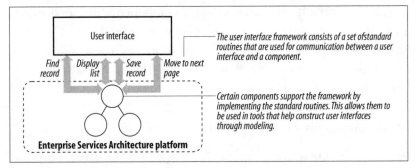

Figure 4-3. User Interface Abstraction Framework

Level 4: Loosely Coupled Components and Services

The loosely coupled components created in Enterprise Services Architecture level 4 offer the most dramatic creation of business value that can be achieved with this approach. A properly designed and constructed set of components can make the difference between a quick reaction to new business conditions and a frustrating wait while retooling takes place under fire. The machinery of components and services created in this level should allow IT architects to answer "yes" more frequently.

The goal is to create a set of components that represent important business objects and functionality. If these components manage the complexity, and present services that provide useful functionality but do not expose that complexity, then assembly or retooling of applications should be easier and faster. It should be harder for the architect to accidentally introduce tight coupling and rigid structures because the complexity on which these connections are based is concealed. The program coordinating all of the components should be smaller, simpler, and have less to keep track of. If done properly, a set of components should allow an application to be modified or reconstructed far more rapidly than a monolithic application in which the component parts are bound together in a complex fashion.

To gain the benefits of loosely coupled components and services, we must solve some difficult design problems. As a result, we divide our discussion into two areas: one that addresses the challenges of designing a component that provides business value, and another about how loose coupling works in practice.

Modular management of complexity

At the beginning of this chapter, we imagined that the company was one big process labeled "Make Money" and, in the discussions of previous Enterprise Services Architecture levels, the implied grouping of objects, services, and processes was at the enterprise application level. The services were built on top of each application through adapters that acted as gateways to the data and functionality within. So far, we have not addressed how components would be constructed other than suggesting that they would be based on APIs offered by the vendors of enterprise applications.

But for Enterprise Services Architecture level 4 to work, we have to be able to create components out of and on top of existing applications. We have to be able to map from one large application to a smaller number of components. We must be able to have an individual component assemble objects and services from many different enterprise applications. If we do not have this flexibility, we are basically stuck with the enterprise application and the services we can build on top of it as the unit of architecture.

The layer that allows the sort of components we will build to exist in the way we have just described is the Enterprise Services Architecture platform. In Chapter 5, we review in greater detail what an Enterprise Services Architecture platform does, but for now we summarize adapters for application services in Figure 4-4.

The Enterprise Services Architecture platform provides the ecosystem in which the components can live. The components need to be able to exist at design time, at configure time, and at runtime. They need to be able to present their services to other components for invocation and to invoke other services. They need their own persis-

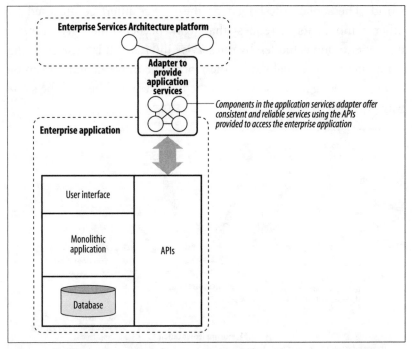

Figure 4-4. Adapter for services from enterprise applications

tent storage for information created by the component, located outside of the underlying enterprise applications. They need to be able to employ the functionality of platform component systems like content management, enterprise application integration, or data warehousing to transform the objects they process. They need a repository for the metadata that describes them.

Component size

The Enterprise Services Architecture platform then presents us with a serious design problem. How large or small should components be to serve our current and future business needs?

This question is crucial because making components too small or too large can reduce their value. To prepare for our explanation of why this is true, we will first delve deeper into the how components work. Figure 4-5 shows the different parts of the component. The service interface is what the component looks like to the outside world. The services described by the service interface are used by other components to request that work be performed. The service implementation is hidden by the service interface. It is the part of the component that actually does the work. The implementation can be changed as long as the services to the outside world behave the same way.

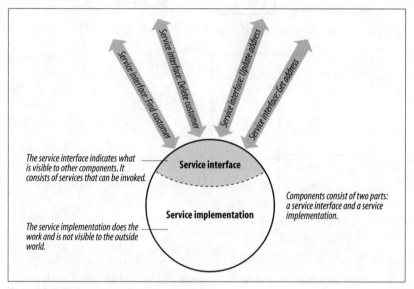

Figure 4-5. Basic component structure

Good examples of the extremes of large and small components are easy to find. At the small end of the spectrum, you can think of each API call as a component. The program to bring these together needs to know a lot about what the small component will do and how to use it properly. The component itself may be simple, but the program that uses it is not (see Figure 4-6).

At the larger end of the component size spectrum is the enterprise application. A CRM application can be thought of as a very large component. The APIs of the CRM application can be thought of as services of that component. The problem is that to use the services, one has to know a lot about the complexity inside the CRM system. It is frequently hard to know all of the side effects that may occur from changing the state of an enterprise application through APIs.

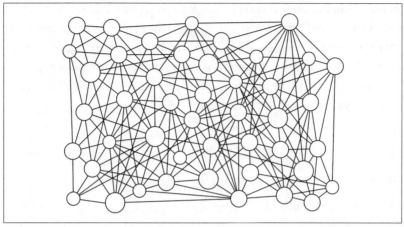

Figure 4-6. Many small components

Whether components are large or small, the complexity is not contained. It is still visible to the architect and must be managed directly (see Figure 4-7).

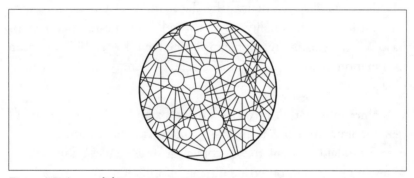

Figure 4-7. A monolithic component

Both cases include a large nest of complexity that must understood as monolith. A monolith is a complex structure that is not organized into smaller parts. When components are too small, the monolith of complexity is the context that needs to be understood to make the component useful. When the components are too large, the monolith of complexity resides inside the component.

Components of the right size capture that complexity in smaller parts that are easier to understand, manage, and reuse. The complexity of a particular object or group of objects is brought together in one component and services are used to communicate what other applications and components need from those objects. The complexity of a specific function or process is captured in separate components. The complexity required to orchestrate the components to do a certain job may be kept in another component. Well-designed components tend to look like Figure 4-8.

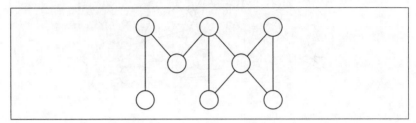

Figure 4-8. Balanced components

Successful components usually have the following characteristics. They tend to be grouped around stable business functions. It is as if islands of stability are defined by the natural relationships of data and business functionality. By "natural" we mean relationships based on the existing relationships in the data. By "stable" we mean information that is part of the essential identity of the business object.

Customer information provides a great example. Customer components, common elements in many enterprise applications, include core information about the customer, such as name, address, telephone number, and other identifying information. Defining a basic component is generally not hard. The question then becomes what additional information should be managed by the component. If you start adding information about a customer's preferences for a particular product to the core component, perhaps you will have to include that core component in a lot of processing that it may not be required for. You end up with a situation in which every transaction references the core customer component. Information that is related to a customer but only germane to a given process (process-related information) should perhaps be housed in a component that manages a certain process and includes all of the information required for that process except what is in the core component. The separation of process-related and process-independent information is one guideline for component design.

The nature of a business process can also serve as a guide to forming components. If a process has a beginning, middle, and an end, it may make sense to have a component dedicated to each phase.

While the right design is hard to describe, the wrong design is easier to recognize. Any of the following indicators may suggest that the component is too large:

- If only a small portion of the internal code is invoked to satisfy any one request
- If the component is involved in everything that happens in an application
- If it is hard to use

The following indicators may mean that a component is too small:

- If it is hard to understand what the component does without knowing a lot about its context
- If it has an identity that is not intuitive
- If it cannot be used by itself

As is the case with any difficult design problem, general guidance is far less useful than experience in implementing and living with design decisions.

Our best definition of a level 4 Enterprise Services Architecture component satisfies the following criteria:

- Lean interface to the functionality.
- Presents a meaningful unit of functionality.
- No semantic dependencies on other components. Components know little about each other. (We will discuss this in more detail in the section on loose coupling.)
- Provides what is needed by business processes.
- Can participate in any process.

- No unintended side effects (a specific requirement for components built on top of other applications).

So if the first job of Enterprise Services Architecture level 4 is to manage the complexity by taking the time to sort it into appropriate components, the second job is to figure out how those components will talk to each other.

Loose coupling

Loosely coupled components can communicate with each other and interact in ways that maintain flexibility. Dependencies are minimized. When they do exist, design them carefully to allow the components on either side of the relationship to evolve. The trick to getting this right is making sure that all of the services offered by all of the components in an architecture provide the right toolkit to do the work of an application. The service interfaces are really the elements that perform the work and pass information back and forth. That is why Yefim Natis, the Gartner analyst cited in Chapter 3, thinks that interface-oriented architecture would be a better name for what most people call service-oriented architecture.

Components are related to each other in two ways: they invoke each others' services, and they refer to information in each other. Loose coupling does not mandate eliminating all dependencies between components. That would be impossible. The goal of loose coupling is to minimize the interaction between components and to describe the interaction in such a way that both sides know what they are expected to give and to get. The precise definition of what a service does is a sort of contract between that component and the rest of the world. The component agrees that anyone who invokes a service with valid data gets a predictable response.

One powerful aspect of this structure is that a component can be upgraded or changed without consultation with the rest of the world as long as the basic contract is kept. The unit of innovation and evolution is smaller. It is easier to create specialized development teams. This stands in sharp contrast to monolithic structures in which it may be impossible to determine the effect of any specific change to the system and upgrades must take place all at once.

The contracts that describe the services are part of the solution, but, in order to succeed in creating loosely coupled components, the contracts must have another feature. The abstractions should not expose any implementation details of a component. Joel Spolsky coined the phrase "leaky abstractions" to describe what happens when implementation details or dependencies suddenly slip out. An abstraction conceals complexity but allows some sort of simplified communication. The abstraction is leaky if some complexity or dependency is accidentally exposed. Consider a component that provides a record from a database, but instead of splitting the fields from the record into five different parameters, it returns them as a tab-delimited string in a specific order. Many parts of the complexity may be hidden, but if the order of the fields is changed or a new field is introduced, the software that relies on this abstraction will break. An implementation detail has leaked out through the abstraction.

The looseness of loose coupling is that there is an end to the chain of dependency. If you follow the code in a monolithic application, in the worst case you may find yourself tracing a never ending chain of data structures and subroutines, all related to each other in different ways with no pattern and no end, spaghetti code that overlaps itself haphazardly.

Loosely coupled components meet the following criteria:

- The contract for each service is explicitly stated and documented.
- Services are designed to minimize interdependencies between components.
- Services are designed to be as stable as they can be while reflecting core underlying relationships.
- The more frequently used a service is, the more stable it is.
- Abstractions hide implementation details and are not leaky.
- The services are described by metadata.

Issues in loosely coupled component architectures

An architecture defined by loosely coupled components is able to accommodate change at the minimum cost and the maximum speed. If a certain change is proposed, it falls into one of two cases: either it affects the services provided by the component or it doesn't. If it doesn't, the change can be made as long as all the services work the same way. If it changes the behavior of a service, all services that use that service must be analyzed to see what effect the change has on them. In any event, the path to determining the scope of a change is highly predictable.

In monolithic systems, it is often impossible to predict how much work a particular change will entail and the effect it will have on particular systems. The fear of facing this unknown slows the rate of evolution of monolithic systems.

Loosely coupled components and services force a comprehensive design process on an architecture. Monolithic systems are created by solving one problem, then solving another, then another, until you have created a behemoth. The monolithic systems that succeed do so because they have some sort of partitioning, some set of rules, that help manage the complexity.

Building an Enterprise Services Architecture of loosely coupled components requires conscious design of a system. Much more work must be done up front to implement a component system. But much less work is done to change it down the road, and much more is possible with such a system.

But just because you create a design doesn't mean that it will be successful. Most designs involve trade-offs relating to the specific context of a system. Making these trade-offs in a way that anticipates future needs is the key skill of a successful designer. We have mentioned some of the trade-offs already, such as the balance between many smaller components and few larger ones. It is generally safer to start with fewer components and decompose the larger ones as the justification for doing so becomes clear.

Another issue that arises early and often when designing components is ownership of the data. In some situations it is best for a component to manage all of the data that it needs for its operations. In other situations, it may be beneficial to have a set of components that own the data and then parcel it out to the components that use and transform it. The optimal structure depends on the specific context.

The design of a set of components also should be informed by the knowledge of which data and relationships are stable and which are likely to change. Moshe Barnes, an expert data and object modeler, generally starts his designs by separating data into process-independent and process-related information. The data then tends to form into stable islands of process-independent information with stable relationships to other process-independent information. These islands are surrounded by groups of process-related information that change much more frequently. The more that something is referred to, the more stable the dependency should be. Process-related dependencies should exist between components at the edge, related to that process. Nests of volatile, rapidly changing components should perhaps be encapsulated within one component. This pattern of design, however, ensures that the most frequently changing information has the smallest possible impact on the system.

In the next section, we propose a still more advanced Enterprise Services Architecture level that deals with process control and configuration. Loosely coupled components and services should anticipate the needs at that level. In the best component design, components participate in a process control abstraction the same way that UI services are designed to operate in a user interface abstraction.

Dynamic systems in high value areas of the business are the largest beneficiaries of loosely coupled components. Flexible systems also need a component now and then. The life cycle of a system is also important here. Because the investment in design is significant, systems that have a short shelf life are probably not ideal targets for componentization.

Level 5: Process Control

In a loosely coupled component architecture, you carve up the complexity into manageable chunks and clearly define the interaction between them. At the center of these components is usually some sort of component that orchestrates the behavior of all of the other components. In Enterprise Services Architecture level 5, we examine the structure of these orchestrating components.

Generally, the component that orchestrates all the others uses the native language provided by the Enterprise Services Architecture platform. If Java is the preferred language for components, the process control will be orchestrated by Java code. The component invokes services from other components, retrieves data, manipulates it, stores it again, and interacts with the user interface as needed. Enterprise Services Architecture level 5 simplifies changing the orchestration processes or the processes within a component.

The Enterprise Services Architecture platform itself provides this capability. Internally, it may use an XML file, a simple scripting language, or possibly one of the new business process control languages such as BPEL4WS or BPML. Processes are represented in different ways. Many systems offer visual configuration of processes. Application forms or order forms are frequently models of processes. Certain components or objects are used to represent processes. All of these approaches have advantages and disadvantages.

Types of processes also differ and the method of expressing them must take that into account. User interface processes are geared toward short-term interaction with a user moving from page to page, entering data, and invoking functionality that changes the application state. Backend processes may run for days or weeks and may wait for several different events to occur before the next step is triggered.

Process control adds a level of configurability to the process within a component. The configurability added in level 5 meets the following criteria:

- Components are built to support a process abstraction.

- The process abstraction has a simplified mechanism for defining the order in which services within the component and the services of other components are invoked.

- The process control services are described by metadata.

The process need not be configurable in real time, although in certain circumstances, such as controlling e-commerce applications, that flexibility may be beneficial. The structure of the adapters used in a framework for process control is shown in Figure 4-9.

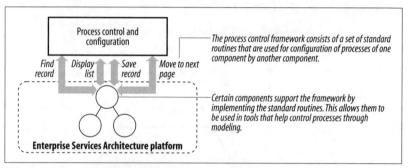

Figure 4-9. Process control framework

This configuration capability may be used to change the behavior of a single component or to rapidly create a set of components that have similar but slightly different behavior.

Such components are likely to be of use only for dynamic systems in which frequent change is a permanent part of market conditions.

How Abstraction Creates Business Value

One simple way to think of all of the levels we have discussed so far is as different flavors of abstraction. Each level grows and builds to some extent on the levels beneath it as shown in Figure 4-10. Each level allows more and more functionality to be optimized or applied to new purposes.

Abstraction does not mean that the impact of change will be zero. When a new function arrives in a system based on Enterprise Services Architecture principles, components may have to change. Interfaces between components may have to change. But the change happens in a way that encourages the design that informed the creation of components to be preserved. In a monolith, a new piece of functionality may be grafted on wherever it fits. In Enterprise Services Architecture, the architect must first determine the right place for this functionality because he or she knows that the system has been designed for flexibility.

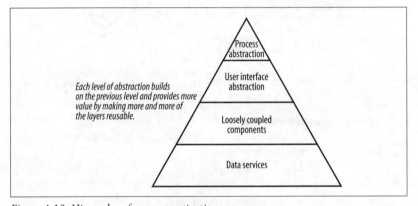

Figure 4-10. Hierarchy of componentization

The business value of abstraction comes out primarily when the business must change. The more a system must change, the more abstraction will provide value. That's why we have a targeted approach. If an architect is sure that a system will not change, there is really no problem with the monolithic approach as long as other systems can get to the data. But if the functionality of an application is relevant to other applications, or the application will need to change, then techniques described in this chapter can turn an enterprise application from a straightjacket into a powerful weapon.

With the different categories of flexibility and Enterprise Services Architecture compliance levels as tools, we can now have a much more sophisticated discussion of what kind of flexibility we require in an application; we refer to these levels throughout the rest of this book. But the flexibility we have described presents many difficult issues and questions. In Chapter 5, we turn to the layer of software that brings together all the components we have discussed so far: the Enterprise Services Architecture platform.

5

The Platform

Ten years ago, almost all applications were monolithic. Ten years from now, most new applications will come with a set of reusable components and services. Between now and then software that we will call the Enterprise Services Architecture platform will enable existing applications to play in a world of components and services.

The Enterprise Services Architecture platform is an extension of the application server platform, which itself was an extension of the operating system. The application server created a variety of higher-level services, application design patterns, and user interface frameworks on top of the operating system that allow application developers to worry more about building their applications and less about the plumbing needed to move data around and process it. The Enterprise Services Architecture platform is like a higher-level application server for a component architecture. It takes care of the plumbing so the architects can worry more about how to craft the components to solve business problems.

Even if we could wave a magic wand and create a set of fully componentized applications, companies would still need an Enterprise Services Architecture platform or the equivalent to provide the ecosystem for components to reflect specific business needs. The platform layer is also needed to create components that aggregate functionality across applications and to support composite applications.

The Enterprise Services Architecture platform is the central hub, the connector that brings together enterprise applications like ERP and

CRM, platform component systems like content management and data warehousing, and new components built using the Enterprise Services Architecture platform.

Early versions of the Enterprise Services Architecture platform have already been announced by a variety of software vendors. The functionality claimed by most boils down to a system that performs the following five tasks:

- Creates an ecosystem for components.
- Brings components built on enterprise applications into the ecosystem.
- Brings functionality from platform component systems into the ecosystem.
- Provides an environment for design time, configure time, and runtime.
- Enables model-driven development.

Figure 5-1 illustrates the moving parts that most Enterprise Services Architecture platforms have to perform these tasks.

The rest of this chapter describes how the Enterprise Services Architecture platform performs its fundamental tasks.

Component Ecosystem

What happens in an ecosystem? Living things are born, grow, struggle for survival, live, and then die. This sums up what an Enterprise Services Architecture platform provides for components. The development framework describes how components are born. Just as animals all tend to have similar body parts, all components in an Enterprise Services Architecture platform share the following common elements:

- Adapters for existing enterprise applications to retrieve data or to invoke services of the applications

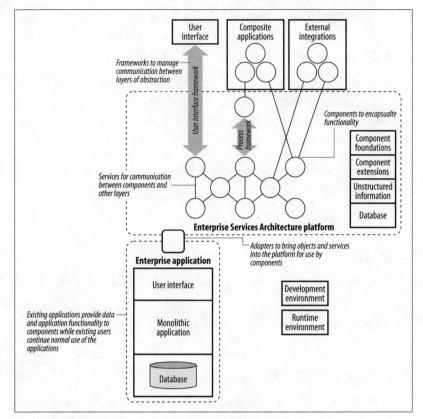

Figure 5-1. Enterprise Services Architecture platform structure

- The ability to invoke functionality from the platform component systems that are part of the Enterprise Services Architecture platform

- The ability to create, inside the Enterprise Services Architecture platform, new components with new functionality that supplement the functionality drawn from existing enterprise applications

- The ability to invoke services from other components

- Support for user interface abstraction frameworks such as portals

- Support for process control abstraction frameworks such as BPEL4WS

- Support for data management to bring together data from underlying enterprise applications into a unified form

- Support for runtime operational features such as service monitoring, load balancing, and usage reporting
- Support for advanced features such as performance tuning, security, transactions, and other functions
- Support for metadata repositories required for model-driven development

Basic Component Features

We start with the basic functions of a component itself. A component is like an object in an application server. It is a container for data and functionality. It has services that can be defined, which are like function calls that other components or programs use to talk with the component. It has data that can be held in the component when it exists in the runtime environment. It has methods, programs that are not visible to other components, that help do the work of the component. It also has the ability to store and retrieve data in a local database. So far this is pretty straightforward.

The two most important elements are the adapters for the enterprise applications and the ability to integrate functionality from platform component systems.

Adapters for enterprise applications

Adapters for enterprise applications provide a gateway to objects (meaning mostly data), services (API calls, XML interfaces, and EAI interfaces), and processes (the rare case in which an enterprise application exposes the execution of a process in a dynamically configurable way). An adapter framework is a set of utility programs and functions that help build adapters a certain way. The adapters themselves are specific programs written to move data back and forth from the application or to invoke services of the application. The adapters are used by the components to bring the enterprise applications into the ecosystem.

Adapters for platform components

The next thing that goes into the component definition is another kind of adapter that provides access to functionality from platform component systems, which are huge toolboxes of functionality for a specific purpose. One of the most prevalent types of platform component systems is the content management system. The adapters to platform component systems allow Enterprise Services Architecture components to use their functionality as part of a component. For example, if a component in a composite application has access to purchase orders from 10 different underlying enterprise applications, the component might use the indexing functions of a content management system to create a searchable index of all of the purchase orders across all of the systems. The component could use functionality from a data warehouse to create various kinds of reports on purchase orders in all of the underlying systems. EAI functionality should be available to talk to systems inside and outside the enterprise. A wide variety of platform component systems will probably be supported in even the leanest Enterprise Services Architecture platform.

Data management utilities

Defining a collection of master data for a company is one of the most difficult tasks architects will face in implementing Enterprise Services Architecture. The proliferation of enterprise applications means that data is distributed all over the applications. Even if we consider only the process-independent data about a customer, assembling the right information from all of the distributed systems is a large challenge.

Application servers started with the ability to create general-purpose programs and then added specific toolkits to help build functionality. Systems for database connectivity like JDBC and ODBC were the first to come along. One of the equivalents to this sort of element in the Enterprise Services Architecture platform will be systems for data management.

Such a system allows the Enterprise Services Architecture platform to create an index of all locations for a specific type of data in all of the underlying applications. For example, most enterprise applications store some sort of customer data. A data management system creates a cross-reference that tracks which customer records reside in which systems. It then has the ability to store some key information from all of those customer records in a central repository, creating a master database of a subset of all customer information for quick access by the Enterprise Services Architecture components. Data distributed across enterprise application systems can be managed in various ways, and the data management support from an Enterprise Services Architecture platform will probably support both data kept in a central repository as well as systems that store only references to distributed data.

User interface abstraction and process control frameworks

Certain components in an Enterprise Services Architecture play the role of ringmaster. They orchestrate the behavior of other components to perform the desired work and manage communication with end users. These components can present custom services of any kind to interact with all sorts of user interfaces or use a programming language to implement a certain process that involves coordinating the work of many different components. Enterprise Services Architecture platforms will probably have a preferred user interface framework, such as a certain portal system or a UI development environment. Utility routines or code that implements the patterns or the UI framework will likely be a part of the functionality available in a component. The same is true for the basic routines involved in supporting a process framework. In both cases, the support provided is code that implements the interface to the framework. The implementation is then filled in by the component. It is conceivable that more than one UI or process framework could be supported as part of an Enterprise Services Architecture platform.

Advanced Dimensions of Enterprise Services Architecture

Creating an ecosystem to support Enterprise Services Architecture components is an enormous task. The Enterprise Services Architecture platform, which provides this infrastructure, has to address many fundamental issues in order to enable construction of components on top of existing systems right now, not five years from now, when many enterprise applications will be delivered as sets of configurable components. Here are some of the practical issues that must be faced squarely.

Performance

Flexibility and performance are a trade-off. Flexible applications are controlled not only by code but by metadata and configuration mechanisms. So instead of just doing what they need to do, they go to a location in a program and look for the description of what they need to do. Elements within flexible programs are frequently described externally using XML files, for example. Abstraction and loose coupling have associated performance costs because information must be transformed from its native form into the form needed for the simplified abstraction. While none of these issues are overwhelming, cumulatively they could have a crippling effect on the speed of an application or service.

Solving performance problems is pivotal to the success of Enterprise Services Architecture. Imagine what would happen if performance were ignored. One poorly performing service in an interconnected system of components could bring other applications to their knees. Several services with mediocre or erratic performance could have a similar effect.

In the real world of enterprise computing, any service must come with a service level. With monolithic applications, the service level is defined for the entire application. Now, as we explain further in Chapter 7, each service or component has its own service level.

A well-known set of optimizations can be applied at a design or operational level. Choosing asynchronous techniques for as much communication between components as possible is one way to ease the performance burden. Caching, connection pooling, and load balancing are other ways of optimizing performance. The challenge will be to add performance enhancements without reducing the flexibility of the component architecture. This trade-off can be answered definitively only in a specific context.

One technique to enhance Enterprise Services Architecture performance involves binding components at startup time. When they are initially loaded, the components would look at the location of the other components that they use. If they were close, meaning on the same physical machine, optimized methods of communication between components would be used. If the components were far away on other machines or across wide area networks, methods of communication such as web services or EAI would be used. Such a technique is not rocket science but offers significant performance gains.

Security

Another massive challenge for the designers and implementers of component architectures and Enterprise Services Architecture platforms is providing proper access control for each component and process. In a monolithic architecture, security is generally managed by controlling access to the application. If security within the application is required, the vendor of the application provides it.

In Enterprise Services Architecture, security becomes the problem of the platform, and access to services is controlled on a much finer-grained level. In addition to application-level security, each component and each service may have its own security profile. This puts an implementation burden on the developer of the Enterprise Services Architecture platform and an administrative burden on IT staff. Given the mission-critical nature of Enterprise Services Architecture applications, this burden cannot be displaced. Security is much less expensive to incorporate during the development phase than to retrofit later.

Transactions

Another issue that it is dangerous to gloss over is how database level transactions are exposed in Enterprise Services Architecture. This complex issue can be solved in a variety of ways. In the J2EE world, the problem is solved by separating the management of the transactions at the database level from the EJB components that process the data and participate in the transaction. A transaction broker manages the work of starting a transaction or telling the database management components to commit or roll back the transaction. This amounts to a structure in which a set of components actually owns the data, and other components extract it from them.

Another approach is to have the component itself manage the transaction. This of course adds complexity to the component, but it avoids having to implement a transaction broker that manages communication about transactions across components.

Standardization and version management

As applications are broken into components, standardization will extend to the component level. Components in the ideal Enterprise Services Architecture platform will be able to support different levels of a standard, perhaps even at the same time. The caller of a service could specify the version of the interface expected, and the component could react accordingly. Such version management features will be particularly important for application vendors who will release multiple components on different life cycles that will need to be able to talk to each other.

Standards will extend in every direction and make life easier for Enterprise Services Architecture platform vendors and those who use them. This process may not happen quickly, but it certainly will happen.

The component foundations we have discussed so far are shown in Figure 5-2.

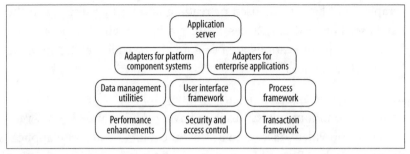

Figure 5-2. Component foundations

Now we will take a closer look at the role enterprise applications and platform component systems play in an Enterprise Services Architecture platform.

Enterprise Applications in an Enterprise Services Architecture Platform

Not all enterprise applications are ready to participate in an Enterprise Services Architecture platform. Some lack the APIs while others have internal structures so complicated that the APIs can't be used safely. Over the next five years, this will change as each new generation of enterprise applications becomes more componentized and ready to live within the Enterprise Services Architecture ecosystem as a set of parts rather than a monolithic whole.

One of the main attractions of the Enterprise Services Architecture platform is that it delivers the benefits of service-oriented architecture before the transformation of the enterprise applications takes place. But in doing its job, the Enterprise Services Architecture platform will run into the limitations of the enterprise applications. Here are the issues that will arise.

The most limiting case is that of an enterprise application or legacy system that was not written to communicate with the outside world. To access the data or functionality of such an application, one has to start at the top or bottom of the application stack. Either screen scraping will have to be used or reading and writing directly to the database. For read-only access, direct access might not be a problem, but such applications are not going to provide significant value beyond data services.

Most enterprise applications are well beyond this worst case in their ability to communicate. Customers have long demanded—and vendors have provided—access to at least the data of enterprise applications through APIs, XML interfaces, EAI messaging, and other import/export mechanisms. Given that most enterprise applications are stable in Enterprise Services Architecture terms, many components in an Enterprise Services Architecture platform are dedicated to providing the sort of data services described in Enterprise Services Architecture level 2.

The last couple of generations of enterprise applications have been built with portal integration in mind. Vendors either supply support for various portal frameworks as part of the application or have supplied adapters for various portals after the fact. The availability of such services generally means that the applications are ready to participate in user interface abstraction. Even if such support is not provided by the vendor, with a robust and well-designed API, an adapter may be constructed.

At Enterprise Services Architecture levels 4 and 5, we run into the limitations of the monolithic architecture of most enterprise applications. Most such applications were constructed from a central core of application functionality that involves manipulating a tightly coupled collection of objects. In CRM applications, the sales order, business partner, and product objects are typically bound up in so many different connections that they are inseparable. In such a situation, it may be impossible to present a component view of the sales order that exposes operations on that object without affecting other tightly bound objects. In cases like these, the ability to expose components is limited by the internal design.

On the other hand, most monolithic applications have been extended over the years, and the extensions are generally separate objects unto themselves that communicate in stable ways with the tightly coupled central objects. These extensions are much more likely to make components easily separable.

Other issues that must be taken into account include the side effects of any API call, which must be well understood, and the performance of any portion of an enterprise application that is exposed. The inescapable cost of the Enterprise Services Architecture platform's componentization of enterprise applications is the presence of the adapter layer, which will have an effect on performance.

Given these realities, it is unlikely that enterprise applications will be broken into a large number of components. It is likely that the number of possible components can be predicted by the number of extensions to the core central components. One component will be defined for the center and one each for the extensions.

Very few enterprise applications that have configurable processes controlled by APIs will work in a process framework. Such process control is likely to be found first in custom components created in the Enterprise Services Architecture platform to support a dynamic application.

Of course, the only reason to define components of enterprise applications is to do useful work, and the limitations mentioned here are significant only if they stand in the way of achieving the desired flexibility. We will look closer at what sort of flexibility is optimal in Chapter 6.

Platform Component Systems in an Enterprise Services Architecture Platform

Platform component systems are the power tools of the Enterprise Services Architecture. Systems for content management, enterprise application integration, knowledge management, data warehousing, portals, business process management, and application development will be incorporated into the Enterprise Services Architecture platform.

Components can have methods from all of the platform component systems and use their repositories for special purposes. It is likely, for example, that many of the Enterprise Services Architecture level 2 data services will use EAI technology to talk to enterprise applications because so much work has been done to expose the data in this manner. Application servers will probably provide the shell to contain the component ecosystem. Data warehouses will likely be used to help implement data management services, and content management, as we mentioned earlier, will index content distributed across enterprise applications.

The key for platform systems is to make sure that fitting them into the Enterprise Services Architecture platform does not dramatically restrict their functionality or introduce performance penalties that make their functionality unusable.

The most common platform component systems are summarized in Figure 5-3.

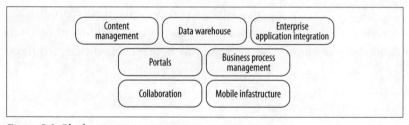

Figure 5-3. Platform component systems

Enterprise Services Architecture Platform Development Framework

The job of the development framework is to provide the tools needed to construct applications that use Enterprise Services Architecture components and deploy them.

The Enterprise Services Architecture platforms that are now appearing are in their early stages. Only a fraction of the functionality we outlined as component foundations and component extensions is available in current versions. With each new generation of the platform, more adapters for enterprise applications and platform component systems will arrive. More objects and services from enterprise applications and more functionality from platform component systems will be at the disposal of architects. This dramatically expands the notion of the platform from the narrow definition of an application server to a much more comprehensive vision of an application server extended to handle content management, data warehousing, enterprise application integration, mobile interfaces, and all the other toolkits.

Evolution of the development, configure time, and runtime environments will also occur as the Enterprise Services Architecture platform matures. The runtime environment will offer performance enhancements and functionality to help manage the increased complexity of the operational environment.

Model-Driven Development

At first, Enterprise Services Architecture platforms will offer development environments that are quite similar to the interactive development environments (IDEs) that come with the current generation of application servers. Over time, Enterprise Services Architecture platforms will put the metadata created to describe components and services to work. The existence of the metadata will dramatically improve on the productivity of traditional development methods and replace them with an approach based on modeling.

In such a world, much less Java code is written. Instead, the developer chooses from a menu of objects that are described in metadata and glues them together. Whether this activity takes place using a simple scripting language or with a fancy visual interface is not important. The impact of such techniques is an increase in the speed of development and the reliability of software. The frameworks we have mentioned for user interface abstraction and process control allow this sort of plug-and-play development. It is likely that the number of frameworks will grow dramatically as new standards for application functionality and integration develop. For example, some day a content management framework will be used to describe all of the basic functions provided by a content management system.

The existence of these advanced development tools will not mean automatic value for every company. They will be like musical instruments: the companies that understand the design principles and build the necessary skills will be able to take full advantage of these powerful tools to create business value like a musician makes beautiful sounds from a violin.

The companies that do not acquire a deeper understanding and proficiency in Enterprise Services Architecture will not find them much use at all. A violin does not play itself.

With our exhausting tour of the internal structure of Enterprise Services Architecture completed, we now turn to an analysis of how we can put this approach to work in the real world, the subject of chapters 6 and 7.

6

Applying Enterprise Services Architecture

Japanese automobile manufacturers practice "lean manufacturing." In lean manufacturing, the automobile manufacturer starts out, rather ironically, with a much larger design team than U.S. automakers use.[*] The reason? Lean manufacturers start with a detailed design process that includes a large multidisciplinary team, many of whom are committed for the life of the project. This core team is under the control of a strong leader who seeks to ferret out all of the major decisions and trade-offs that will arise in the design and manufacture of the new automobile. As the production of the car moves through the pipeline, the size of this team shrinks as the main activity shifts from design and planning to execution.

In the mass production paradigm often used by U.S. automakers, the design team starts small and then, as the project progresses, adds people from various disciplines. In the mass production model, the team becomes the largest and the most diverse just before the car enters production. At that time the contradictions in the design are addressed and the difficult trade-offs are made. Resolving problems at this stage costs more, takes much longer, and requires many more people. Expanding the team also introduces delays; as people join the team, they must be brought up to speed on the project.

---

[*] See *The Machine That Changed The World: The Story of Lean Production* by Womack et al (HarperCollins), p. 115.

The difference between the two approaches is dramatic. The lean manufacturing approach results in a significant competitive advantage. In the lean manufacturing model, the design period is 20 percent less and requires only about 60 percent of the engineering time compared to the mass production model.[*]

Enterprise Services Architecture: Lean Manufacturing for IT

Enterprise Services Architecture is, in essence, the lean manufacturing model applied to IT architecture. The goal of the Enterprise Services Architecture process is to force a comprehensive design up front using a team that has all the information it needs to make the key decisions and manage the trade-offs. The system categories (stable, flexible, and dynamic) and the compliance levels described in Chapter 4 are tools used in the design process.

But IT infrastructure is not a car. Important differences between creating a forward-looking IT architecture and manufacturing automobiles lead to both problems and opportunities.

The malleability of software is a curse in the sense that it allows poor design to work. When a system is created to solve one problem, with no regard to how it may evolve, and then adapted to solve another problem, and then another, the result is a monolithic application that serves some purposes but is impossible to adapt. Monoliths are created because, at some point, getting work done in the present overshadowed the goal of preparing a flexible, consistent architecture that is adaptable for future needs. If you designed a car this way, it would be impossible to build.

The malleability of software, however, provides tremendous opportunities. Unlike an automobile, where building a steering wheel is not useful without the rest of the car, in IT, a part of the system may be quite useful and in many cases deployed without the rest of the

---

[*] Ibid, p. 118.

system in place. Software components that are loosely coupled through well-designed abstractions can also be replaced much more easily than swapping out an engine or a transmission.

In this chapter, we review the comprehensive design—"the big think"—that takes place at the beginning of the Enterprise Services Architecture process. We look at the beginning, middle, and end of the big think and point out what sort of analysis and questions are most beneficial along the way. We describe the shape of a successful process rather than a strict set of steps. That said, some of our recommendations are quite specific.

The Enterprise Services Architecture process divides the big think into four steps:

1. Research
2. Forecasting
3. Design
4. Implementation

The goal of the big think is to find out where Enterprise Services Architecture's flexibility should be applied to provide the most value for the business now and in the future. What kind of components do we need and in what order should we build them? At the end of this analysis, the company should have a plan for how each application will evolve and how they will all work together in an Enterprise Services Architecture platform.

Fear of the Big Design Project

Embarking on such a process may generate some trepidation. Most IT veterans have suffered through redesign projects that have gone nowhere and led to nothing. Why should Enterprise Services Architecture be different?

Two common flaws prevent the completion of a large design project. Some efforts never end because they attempt to go into too much detail. Instead of sorting out the major parts of the system and how they will be connected, they try to specify everything. Another mistake is avoiding hard decisions. Most of us have been involved in projects that have lurched back and forth between two incompatible paths without coming to a decision.

Like other approaches such as the Rational Unified Process, Scrum, and eXtreme Programming, which we describe further in Chapter 7, Enterprise Services Architecture attempts to move rapidly toward a completed design through humility and constant awareness that any major design is an iterative process.

If architects think their first version of the big think is supposed to be correct, they will be embarrassed to change it later. To succeed, we must design knowing that we will learn along the way. The design of a large IT infrastructure is a gigantic undertaking and can be perfected only through a succession of versions. The design team should also be aware that the design will be implemented incrementally and that additional relevant information will become available after deployment.

Enterprise Services Architecture should not be thought of as a big bang. It is a big think that never stops, followed by a lot of little bangs. Enterprise Services Architecture should happen every day: when upgrading a system, when choosing a new enterprise application, and when creating a custom application. Keeping Enterprise Services Architecture in mind while directing such activities enables the flexibility we have outlined so far.

As the Enterprise Services Architecture process unfolds, gradually more and more flexibility is created, more components become available, more composite applications become possible, and more operational skills are developed. And one day a company ends up in an Enterprise Services Architecture end-state that puts it ahead of the game.

In this chapter, we explore how to perform the big think. In the next, we look at how to create a plan to gradually implement it through a stream of manageable projects that provide information about whether the architecture was right.

The Shape of an Enterprise Services Architecture Implementation

To prepare ourselves for learning more about the process of finding where to apply Enterprise Services Architecture, we will first explain the general shape of an Enterprise Services Architecture implementation. What we mean by shape is the broad stages in which an Enterprise Services Architecture grows.

The order of the Enterprise Services Architecture compliance levels described in Chapter 4 is not rigid. Level 1 concerns how well a company understands its architecture while levels 2 through 5 describe features of the architecture.

In practice, though, the order in which Enterprise Services Architecture is implemented is actually pretty well described by the order of the levels. The data services of level 2 and the user interface abstraction of level 3 happen in parallel. Sometimes people put a portal in place to protect the users from seeing the changes that happen underneath. In other situations, integration between applications is more important than new user interfaces, and data services are created to support easier integration by components. In this case, the user interface layer for new composite applications may come later. This configuration is shown in Figure 6-1.

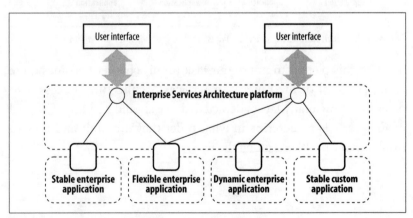

Figure 6-1. UI abstraction, a frequent first stage

Generally significant amounts of loosely coupled components are built after data services and user interface abstraction is in place. These components become the foundation for composite applications or flexible integrations.

Process abstraction is generally the last sort of flexibility in an Enterprise Services Architecture implementation. Process abstraction relies on the loosely coupled components supporting some sort of process framework that allows their behavior to be controlled at a higher level by a scripting language or metadata. All of these moving parts are shown in Figure 6-2.

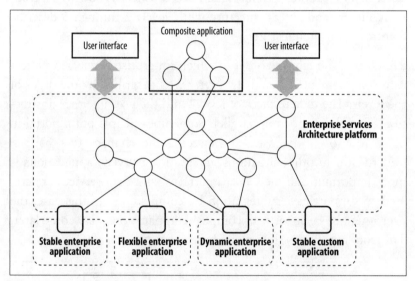

Figure 6-2. A complete Enterprise Services Architecture implementation

So, with this picture in mind, our task in this chapter becomes quite clear. The goal of the Enterprise Services Architecture process is to determine how many layers depicted above should be built. The goal of Chapter 7 is to describe in what order they are built and how to troubleshoot problems along the way.

Assessing Your Starting Point

The research stage of the Enterprise Services Architecture process assembles detailed information required for a good design. In this stage, we document the flexibility of the current systems using compliance levels as a guide, map out the important data in those systems, and analyze the essential processes that create value.

The research stage begins with an assessment of the current state of a company's systems and an analysis of how those systems support the business. Completing this assessment is the definition of meeting Enterprise Services Architecture level 1. It provides a clear understanding of the starting point.

The analysis of current systems determines the expense of meeting the various Enterprise Services Architecture compliance levels. Most enterprise applications have a method of reading data, some have APIs that allow data to be written safely, and increasingly they come with adapters for participation in portals. Some of these features may be available only in the latest version of the products, not the ones currently installed. Custom legacy applications may have none of these attributes.

This analysis should include a description of each system along with a rough estimate of how long it would take the system to get to each of the Enterprise Services Architecture compliance levels, or a determination that it would not be possible—or profitable—to get to a certain level.

Understanding the data used in key business processes is the next step. This step is not a mindless collection of every field in every application, which is relatively easy to do and quite useless. The goal is rather to start to understand the core data of the enterprise and find the core objects that are used repeatedly in different applications. The usual suspects are customer, sales order, business partner, product, part, and so on. The analysis should identify which parts of each object are in which application. Where is core information duplicated? Where does information become incompatible?

The research into these first two topics in the Enterprise Services Architecture stage 1 analysis provides the foundation for the most difficult part: analyzing which processes are key to creating value in the business.

At most companies, processes are not well understood. Senior executives asked to list the most important processes provide widely divergent answers. Most people think about processes from an operational level. Order to cash—the process that an order goes through from the day it is created to the day that the cash arrives from the customer—is often mentioned as the classic example. Other commonly understood processes include qualifying customers into segments for marketing, fulfilling an order, or handling a change request.

Most of these processes take place within the boundaries of the organization. But to have an impact on the design, the analysis of process must not be bound by tradition. Processes that have not yet been automated must also be examined.

The new frontier for automation includes a variety of processes: processes for strategic decision-making, collaborative processes, and processes that cross boundaries between functions in an enterprise and between companies. A survey may not mention these processes, yet they can be crucial to creating value and Enterprise Services Architecture enables their automation.

Processes must be categorized by their stability. The same categories used for applications—stable, flexible, and dynamic—can be applied to processes. Operational processes tend to be stable while strategic and collaborative processes tend to be less stable. Cross-functional and cross-enterprise processes may fall into either category.

When all three steps are complete, the combination of the compliance level for each system, the data, and the processes creates a detailed picture of a company's systems. With such an analysis in hand, a variety of tasks become easier, including constructing composite applications, planning integrations, automating supplier relationships, integrating applications, or determining the cost of creating interfaces for customers. It also helps in evaluating the potential impact of a new application.

Of course, this analysis can proceed in any order. One can start with processes, move on to data, and finish with analysis of Enterprise Services Architecture compliance levels. Like most large analytical tasks, it is performed in several phases: a first pass to understand the scope of each part of the analysis and raise questions, followed by more research into each area, followed by a simplified view. Toward the end of this analysis, ideas for components and abstractions will start to occur spontaneously. The temptation to rush to design must be resisted until the team completes the forecast of how conditions will change.

Architecture as a Prediction

In the forecasting stage of the Enterprise Services Architecture process, the architects make or analyze predictions about changing business conditions so that future needs can inform the design of the architecture.

Forecasting for a successful IT architecture is similar to a professional golfer preparing for a tournament. One way that a golfer prepares is by practicing fundamentals. An endless succession of practice rounds, hours on the driving range, and lots of time spent putting are all part of the preparation. The other sort of preparation involves a specific golf course. During the practice rounds, golfers try to imagine what kind of shots they might need to get out of trouble or take advantage of a lucky break. They then practice these specific shots so that, under pressure during the tournament, they will be ready to execute.

The architecture designed using the Enterprise Services Architecture process should have both sorts of elements as well. Some of the design decisions should be driven purely by fundamentals of good design. Systems should be encapsulated at an appropriate level to avoid unnecessary dependencies and to allow for change with as little trauma as possible.

The architecture must also incorporate the specific sorts of flexibility that might be required based on how business conditions are likely to change. This is the equivalent of the golfer's special shots, the notion of architecture as a prediction of challenges to come.

These predictions, of course, relate to how the business will grow and evolve. New suppliers may be coming into the market, and the architecture may need to be prepared so that new relationships can be automated quickly. A period of innovation may be coming to an end, which might make the need to support new services less important than reducing costs. The opposite might be true. Government regulations may require more detailed reporting, and making such reporting as inexpensive as possible may provide an advantage.

The ideal situation is one in which the focus on fundamentals keeps improving the general condition of a company's architecture and the side bets, the work done to provide flexibility to prepare for specific problems, actually turn out favorably. Certain types of flexibility often have beneficial uses that cannot be predicted.

With future needs in mind, we now turn to the last preparatory step before the design phase: figuring out where to incorporate flexibility to simplify modifying and optimizing key value-creating processes as business conditions change.

Where Is Flexibility Needed?

If the program presented so far has been followed with even a moderate effort, the resulting analysis will be a powerful tool for managing the IT department.

A company should have the following assets in hand after the research and forecasting steps of the Enterprise Services Architecture process:

- A detailed understanding of the flexibility of each of its systems, defined in terms of Enterprise Services Architecture compliance
- An estimate of the cost of increasing the flexibility of each system

- An understanding of the core data objects of the enterprise and how each system contributes to them

- An understanding of the core processes of the enterprise and how they are supported by the existing systems

- A forecast of how business conditions are likely to change and put new demands on the IT architecture

Creating a catalog of the gaps between the capabilities of the existing systems and the current and future needs of the enterprise is the next step in the Enterprise Services Architecture process. Like any complex design process, this stage is iterative, involving a series of questions to find certain kinds of problems and to uncover potential opportunities for the application of Enterprise Services Architecture.

Finding Enterprise Services Architecture Opportunities

The questions that we will ask to find opportunities for Enterprise Services Architecture are:

- Where is the IT department being sidestepped by business units seeking more flexibility and a faster response?

- Is there a mismatch between the flexibility of current processes and the systems that support them?

- Are there any stable processes that are likely to become more dynamic in the future?

- Are there any processes that are important to value creation that are not supported by systems or supported only to a limited extent?

- Are there cross-functional processes that could be fully or partially automated to provide significant business value?

- Are there strategic decision-making processes that could be fully or partially automated to provide significant business value?

The first question about bypassing the IT department brings up some well-known points of pain. This question identifies friction points that cause frustration in a company or hurt the company's competitive position. In many cases, the business unit has communicated its needs to the IT department, which has not had the ability or capacity to react. Enterprise Services Architecture may or may not provide a way to satisfy the needs of the users. At the very least, Enterprise Services Architecture usually provides a way to help a little and demonstrate business value that can unlock further investment.

The next question looks for mismatches between the present and the future. It examines the boundary between the applications and the processes they are supporting. Is the application automating only part of the process when it could provide more help? Is there manual data collection or other inefficiencies that might be automated? Is an application being used less and less with other mechanisms, such as email and spreadsheets, filling in the gaps?

The analysis should anticipate future needs. Are new demands likely to be made on a given application? What new processes will be brought into the company? What processes will change? What changes will the company want to initiate with suppliers? What changes are business partners going to foist on the company? The ideal candidates for more componentization are key processes for creating value that are likely to undergo significant change.

The last three questions look for important processes that are ripe for automation. The idea is to rethink what processes should be automated given the power of Enterprise Services Architecture to assemble data, manage collaboration, and reuse existing functionality. With this foundation, Enterprise Services Architecture can then add new functionality through composite applications for a targeted audience. In answering these questions we are looking for new opportunities to expand the scope of automation through the power of Enterprise Services Architecture.

In asking these questions, the trail of analysis may involve revisiting work done in the previous stages. Assumptions may need to be verified, forecasts confirmed, and estimates made more exact. As with any large problem, the scope of potential research quickly outstrips the available capacity. The focus of the analysis should always stay close to the processes that are key to creating value.

Answering these questions should produce suggestions, ideas, and tasks for improving systems, such as:

- Creation of adapters that increase the Enterprise Services Architecture compliance of a system and enhance its support for the creation of components or composite applications
- Suggestions for improved business processes
- Ideas for components and services that would be widely reused
- Ideas for new composite applications
- Ideas for new custom applications
- Upgrade of current enterprise applications
- Replacement or retirement of enterprise or custom applications

This list of ideas becomes the requirements for the design stage, as described in the next section.

Different Ways to Focus

Choosing the right focus for a company's resources is an art more than a science. We have outlined a process-centric view of a company's systems that attempts to target the most beneficial areas for investing in improved architecture. The guidelines provide a skeleton that can give a company an idea of how to get started. But this is just one point of view. It may be useful to look at how other analysts have approached this issue.

Geoffrey Moore, a strategy consultant and venture capitalist well-known for his book *Crossing the Chasm* (HarperBusiness), approaches this issue using the concepts of core and context activities. Core activities differentiate a company from its competitors and are key levers of value. Better performance in core activities results in a more successful company and a higher stock price. Context activities are those that are requirements but not differentiators. Context activities are pass/fail. Doing an excellent job in them does not result in more profits or increased revenue. In his book *Living on the Fault Line* (HarperBusiness), Moore provides an analysis of how to differentiate core from context activities. He points out that in rapidly changing markets, core activities differentiate for a while, but then become the industry standard and are transformed to context activities.

Another approach to determining where to focus comes from Fred Crawford and Ryan Matthews, two consultants affiliated with Cap Gemini Ernst & Young. In their book *The Myth of Excellence* (Crown Publishing), they propose a model that describes commercial transactions in terms of price, product, access, experience, and service. They argue that a company should pick one activity in which to dominate with excellent performance, another in which to differentiate with above average performance, and should perform at an industry average level for the rest. Wal-Mart, for example, dominates on price and differentiates on product while Nordstrom dominates on service and differentiates on experience. The goal is to focus a company's resources on areas that will produce the most return.

Once the focus for the enterprise has been determined, research into Enterprise Services Architecture generally reveals a wealth of opportunities. It would be a mistake to see better IT architecture as a panacea, however. A thorough analysis reveals many other problems that go beyond the scope of architecture. IT architecture cannot solve basic problems like undercapacity (too much work to do) or a lack of resources (not enough money available). Political or historical barriers may also hinder progress. While many of these problems may be more important than architecture, Enterprise Services Architecture will at least help figure out the best way to apply the available resources given the other limits placed on the enterprise.

Like most analysis in business books, this analysis is neat and tidy. We do not mean to be glib, but rather to provide a way to focus resources to achieve the maximum benefit from IT. Business value and flexibility are concepts like Mom and apple pie: it is hard to argue against increasing business value and flexibility. The core value from IT, however, comes from actually getting this right, from finding ways of moving information around so that people have what they need to do a better job. This is the goal of IT.

Designing for Flexibility

After all of this self-examination, ideally a company discovers that its systems are already in the Enterprise Services Architecture end-state. The to-do list generated in the last step of the Enterprise Services Architecture process is empty. The architecture in such an ideal state would perfectly match the flexibility of the company's business processes and the way that business conditions will change those processes in the future.

Another extreme scenario is the case where the systems are more flexible than is required. In this case, a company might then hide some of that flexibility through components that simplify the management of the architecture.

Most likely, however, the current architecture is lacking in flexibility in certain crucial areas. Now the fun begins. How do we figure out the right moves that will improve the flexibility of the systems just enough to provide the maximum business value?

To start out, we examine the proposals generated in previous stages of the Enterprise Services Architecture process and sort them according to their potential benefit. The focus should be on the projects at the center of the value-creating processes: those that can save money or those that can increase revenue. It is likely that the moves needed to solve the problems for the most important projects will also have an effect on some smaller issues that could be fixed at the same time. Once a short list has been created, Enterprise Services Architecture compliance levels should be examined to see which one would be able to help.

For example, the high-tech manufacturer mentioned in Chapter 2 found that its booking, billings, and backlog (BBB) reporting was made more accurate and timely by using some data services, at Enterprise Services Architecture level 2, to allow a data warehouse to harvest the information from these applications, and then building reporting and analysis components on top. The annual effort this company spent assembling employee compensation reports was replaced with a one-time creation of data services to allow the data to be pulled into a composite application that could assemble reports in real time. Neither of these examples will be written up in IEEE journal articles about the complexity of computing but both provided substantial business benefits. The high-tech manufacturer's consolidation of the 14 screens into 1 for updating project status is another mundane but highly valuable application of Enterprise Services Architecture. This solution is an example of Enterprise Services Architecture level 3, user interface abstraction, that allowed the services underneath the 14 screens to be accessed and streamlined into 1 user interface.

Enterprise Services Architecture level 4 is usually applied in a larger project that entails creating a composite application. Grainger and eBay have an office equipment liquidation system that links it into the existing systems of a company so that equipment can be disposed of efficiently and at the best price. Developing this system involved constructing components that supported a complex cross-company integration and a composite application inside each company.

Enterprise Services Architecture level 5 is appropriate when certain parts of the context are quite stable, but the process that controls them must be adaptable.

The rule for the design should in general mimic the eXtreme programming maxim of designing to solve the current problem. Our recommendation is a soft version of this principle, however, because if future needs can be foreseen, we believe that it makes sense to make a prediction and invest in some flexibility.

The general principles of Enterprise Services Architecture design are quite simple:

- Choose the most inexpensive and easiest way to achieve the flexibility needed to solve the problem.

- Expose services to connect components in the most loosely coupled manner possible, using abstractions to hide complexity.

- Make modest side bets to support future needs.

The right amount of flexibility is hard to define in the abstract. One positive indicator is that the IT department is not seen as a bottleneck anymore and is included early in analysis and planning.

Other indicators include the coupling of an architectural vision ("Where we are going?") with a forecast of business conditions. Any IT move must be motivated by adding business value. Just because a component is an abstraction does not mean it is a good investment.

Enterprise Services Architecture Skill-Building

If we look at the before and after scenario of most Enterprise Services Architecture implementations, we can see that the changes have a certain shape. The useful parts of the monolithic applications are exposed. Data, application logic, and UIs all sprout up as services. Adapters expose the innards of applications. Components are formed out of all of these parts. With the increase in moving parts and flexibility, new skills will be needed.

In Chapter 7, we take a close look at the way the operations department must change to manage the new complex reality. Components and loose-coupling make changing applications easier and less costly, but they make operations more complicated.

Change management is another new skill that organizations must learn in order to deal with a fully developed Enterprise Services Architecture. In Enterprise Services Architecture, the behavior of applications will be much easier to change, especially if a system implements a process abstraction. Many of the common visions of process flexibility are unrealistic in that they envision a world in which a business analyst looks at a gorgeous graphical UI and changes the way a company does business with a couple of clicks.

This is not realistic for a variety of reasons. Process changes must be communicated to all those involved. Their impact on other systems must be evaluated. The goal is that the bounding condition is not IT, but that doesn't mean that change will be instantaneous in other regards.

In this chapter, we have covered the process of preparing for and executing the big think, the overall plan that provides a comprehensive vision for Enterprise Services Architecture at a company. But plans are useless unless they are deftly executed. In the next chapter, we turn our attention to figuring out how to craft a successful implementation plan and address the practical challenges inherent in making Enterprise Services Architecture a reality.

7

Creating a Road Map

At the end of the big think described in the last chapter, the architectural team should have a clear vision of how the Enterprise Services Architecture end-state would look at their company.

Design, especially at a high level, is so much fun. It is thrilling to solve the puzzle of IT architecture, to imagine a perfect architecture that would meet the needs of everyone in a company, to give each department exactly what it wants. It is a pity the distance between the perfect vision and a working system is always so long.

Wise architects realize that no matter how much work goes into constructing the ideal architecture, it is certain to be wrong in some important ways. A thousand years in front of a whiteboard could find only a fraction of the problems. To really find out how flawed any plan is, one must actually do something about it.

Von Molke, a famous thinker in military history, once observed that "No plan survives contact." For Enterprise Services Architecture, no plan can be of any value unless we make contact with reality through implementation. The perfect vision is of no value to the company; only working software can make a difference. The faster a company brings a design to life, the faster the vision will improve and the more value will be created.

Many of the lessons of this chapter are inspired by insights from agile development methods like eXtreme Programming and Scrum. Others come from larger scale methodologies like the Rational Unified Process™ or the Capability Maturity Model™. The goal is not to be an advocate for any of these methods, but rather to show many different ways to make small steps toward implementing a comprehensive design.

In this chapter, we describe the problems that arise in planning and implementing Enterprise Services Architecture and how to make adjustments after contact. We will look at different ways of organizing the big picture, explain principles for determining stages and milestones, review likely problems, analyze the kind of learning that will take place along the way, and discuss what kind of organizational support will help make an Enterprise Services Architecture implementation successful.

Implementation Scenarios

A variety of factors influence the plan for implementing Enterprise Services Architecture. How big of a mess are you in? How much control and agreement do the implementers have? How well will the user community adapt to change? How well will the operations team be able to support a new system? How much money is available?

Many books have been written about methodology and we have our favorites. For larger projects with hundreds of people, the Rational Unified Process is an excellent method to manage complexity. For a company paralyzed by dysfunctional decision-making processes, the Scrum plan for improving the relationship between managers and development teams is a sure way out. If you know what to do, but cannot build software that is reliable and adaptable, then eXtreme Programming can help.

But no methodology can guarantee the optimal shape for your systems. Methodologies help you execute on the right thing and avoid errors, but there is always plenty of room for judgment calls. The architect must decide on the appropriate next step. Any vision of the future is wrong. It is a question of degree.

So with this humble, if somewhat gloomy, point of view, how can we move forward in any direction to get the maximum benefit?

In the last chapter, we looked at the shape of the plan and we researched the cost of bringing each part of the system up to various levels of Enterprise Services Architecture compliance. In Chapter 6 we showed how the different layers fit together in a fully developed end-state. Now we will look at some scenarios that take different approaches to fulfilling the plan. In doing so, we hope to expand the notion of what a component is or can be.

Scenario 1: Put Up a UI Umbrella and Clean Up Underneath

In this scenario, a new user interface (UI) is introduced to the user community and gradually more and more applications are migrated over to it. The new UI acts as an abstraction layer, encapsulating the systems underneath. Once in place, the underlying delivery mechanisms of the applications are less and less visible. This should eventually allow change to take place with very little impact on the user. The expansion of this UI layer is made possible by adapters that present data and application services from enterprise applications. As more and more adapters become available, more opportunities for creating composite applications arise.

This scenario is basically a straight-up implementation of a portal, followed by a componentization of the enterprise applications as appropriate to the needs of the business. To make this clear, we will work though what each step forward in such a scenario would look like. Let's start with a standard set of enterprise applications, as shown in Figure 7-1.

This figure shows a typical configuration at many companies: enterprise applications wired together with some EAI-based integration. The first step is to add data adapters to the applications and to bring the data together in read-only form in a portal so that new interfaces can be assembled to meet the needs of user groups and expand the reach of the enterprise applications. Such an implementation would look like Figure 7-2.

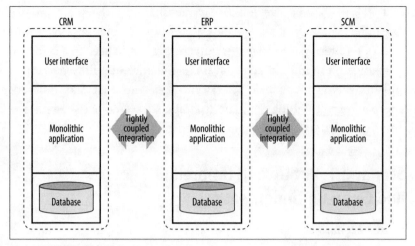

Figure 7-1. Typical enterprise architecture

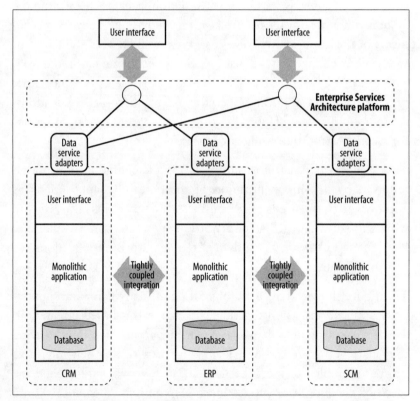

Figure 7-2. UI based on data services

The next step is to determine what kind of flexibility is needed to support some simple new applications. If we bring management of unstructured data into the picture and create a couple of components, we can extend the portal to better support cross-functional and strategic processes. Such a configuration looks like Figure 7-3.

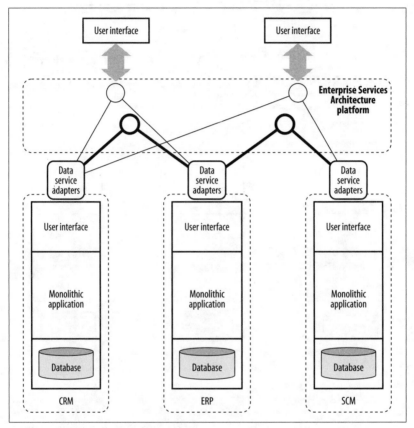

Figure 7-3. Component-based integration

The full implementation of this scenario requires adding more and more components and replacing the stovepipe integrations with integrations based on components. In this scenario, the full benefit of composite applications is unlocked. As more and more components are added, constructing new composite applications becomes easier (although the operational burden grows and change control procedures must manage more complexity). After a critical mass of components is in place, it is possible to introduce process abstraction to help construct composite applications, as we see in Figure 7-4.

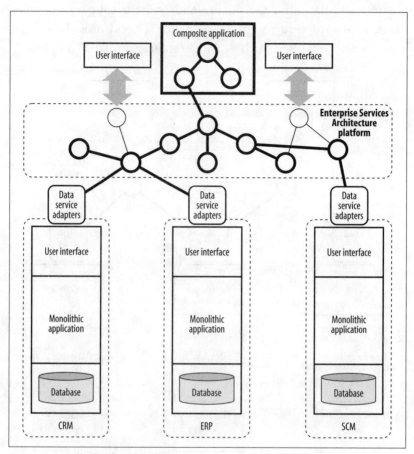

Figure 7-4. Fully developed architecture

This scenario represents the most obvious progression of Enterprise Services Architecture. If a company had a lot of stovepipe integrations that were hampering flexibility, it might make sense to start with data adapters and replace the stovepipe integrations with integrations based on components in the Enterprise Services Architecture platform. If a company identified a need for a compelling composite application with a tremendous benefit, it might make sense to start with that and grow outward. Variations on this approach may make sense in particular situations.

We will now turn to a couple of scenarios that show different ways of thinking about components.

Scenario 2: Use Enterprise Applications as Components

In many companies, mergers are executed as financial transactions. Not until years later are the operational aspects of the merger resolved. The landscape for IT architecture looks like an untended garden of systems, with lots of different parts that do not really work together.

In this situation, the starting point may be quite a mess. Simply reducing the number of moving parts and creating some uniformity represents a significant victory. Each enterprise application that can be discarded means significant savings in hardware, maintenance, and support costs. Consistent implementation of applications can make assembling information from divisions much less expensive.

The various abstraction layers of Enterprise Services Architecture can help organize and implement a gradual approach to simplifying such an architecture. But so far, we have thought of components as living in a development environment, as if a programmer were writing code to create components. Indeed, this will be the most common way that components and services come to life. But here we are expanding our definition to include any consistent group of functionality as a component.

In this scenario, we work through the process of simplifying a fragmented architecture by using enterprise applications as a component layer. During a merger and acquisition, the heterogeneous mess in each company is first migrated to a consistent set of enterprise applications. While this is happening, the groundwork for further progress into a more advanced Enterprise Services Architecture is laid.

Figure 7-5 shows a typical post merger mélange of applications.

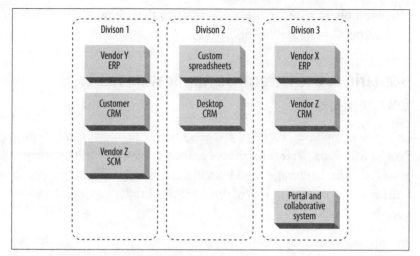

Figure 7-5. Diverse enterprise applications

This simplified view of the diversity of three divisions shows the problems inherent in merging companies. Across the three divisions are three approaches to ERP (two from vendors, one custom system that uses spreadsheets), three different CRM systems, and different levels of adoption of systems such as portals.

In this scenario, the enterprise applications become the components into which all of this diversity is rationalized. Either the best ERP system currently at the company is selected and others are migrated to it, or a new one is chosen for everyone. The same can happen for the other applications as shown in Figure 7-6.

This scenario makes sense as a way to improve things in large organizations where it may be difficult for everyone to agree. Generally, in this scenario, a portion of the application is declared as standard and is implemented uniformly across all divisions. In some cases, one instance of an application may be shared across divisions. Each division can then add specific functionality to the standard implementation to meet its needs. Products can be chosen based not only on functionality but also on the availability of resources to help with implementation and customization.

Some companies turn this into a playbook for executing mergers. After a large manufacturer of industrial power equipment makes an

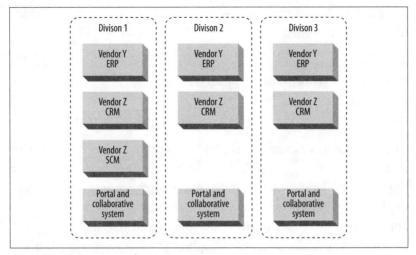

Figure 7-6. Enterprise applications as components

acquisition, its first action is to implement the financial applications it has standardized on.

With such consistent implementations of enterprise applications in place it is then possible to start the process outlined in scenario 1 and further expand automation.

This approach clearly makes sense to a certain set of companies. Adolf Allesch, a senior consultant at Cap Gemini Ernst & Young who described this approach for this book, has put it to work in many engagements.

For our purposes, the interesting question is: Is this approach legitimately Enterprise Services Architecture? We argue that it is essentially Enterprise Services Architecture for the following reasons.

Enterprise Services Architecture is about increasing abstraction. In this approach, the enterprise application, while it may be a large, gangly component that may even have a monolithic structure, is simpler and a better abstraction than the heterogeneous enterprise applications assembled in the merger.

Arguably, the central office and each division are loosely coupled through the standardized portion of the enterprise application. The complexity that handles the specific needs of each division is hidden from the central office.

Whether or not the API is easy to use, after implementation of this approach one consistent set of services can be used to access data. And when work is done to create higher-level services, the standard implementation makes services available for all of the divisions.

The point of this example is that one should not be too orthodox or extreme in thinking that Enterprise Services Architecture can be implemented only by an army of object-oriented programmers and application architects. Enterprise Services Architecture can be applied as a matter of degree, and a component is something that improves abstraction and loose coupling and helps manage complexity to provide business value. Anything that helps do that in IT architecture fits within the broader definition of Enterprise Services Architecture.

While this approach clearly has some advantages, it probably isn't cheap. New software must be licensed, implemented, and customized, although these costs are partially offset by retiring systems. A company must decide on a standardized application. Investment in existing systems must be discarded, one way in which this approach is contrary to the specific value of Enterprise Services Architecture that aims to maximize the value of current systems. In the next scenario, we will look at a way to integrate a heterogeneous environment based on standard services.

Scenario 3: Decentralized Systems Integrated Through Standard Services

In many companies, the divisions, whether or not they were assembled through mergers, are thought of as components and are given great autonomy to do whatever they want as long as they provide certain information and a steady stream of profits.

In this scenario, we look at the problem of a heterogeneous set of existing systems through a different lens. Instead of specifying the implementation of systems in a division, we think of the division from the corporate point of view and ask what that division must provide to the central office.

This approach is taken by most industry standards-setting bodies. Each sort of company in an industry is reduced to an abstraction that provides various services to the intercompany processes that are generally the focus of standards.

What happens, in essence, is that the unification that occurred by virtue of adopting standard enterprise applications now takes place through standard services, as shown in Figure 7-7.

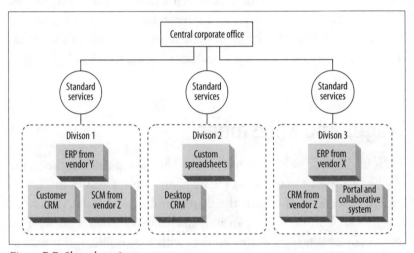

Figure 7-7. Shared services

When the corporation wants to get information or to invoke a process in a division, it uses these standard services. This scenario is quite popular for the exchange of standard data like customer records. When a customer record is created at one division, that fact can be broadcast to the rest of the division or to a central master repository of customer information. The same might be true of financial information. A service might be defined that allows the central office to query certain information about the financial condition of a division.

The advantage of this approach compared to the last is that the implementation is left completely to the divisions. They can provide the services however they would like to. The problem comes in the amount of design and implementation that may have to be done to provide the services. When the services are simple, this is not a large problem. To provide an entire quarterly balance sheet, a rather large detailed definition must be provided, however, and the divisions must find a way to implement it. In the case of using the enterprise applications as the component, the data and services are defined and implemented by the product.

Either scenario 2 or scenario 3 may make sense in the context of an Enterprise Services Architecture implementation, depending on the circumstances. We present them here as an indication of the different approaches one may take when deciding on the details of a particular design.

Stages and Milestones

So far in this discussion, we have looked at the big picture, the shape of what we want to achieve in the long term. In the rest of this chapter, we descend deeper into the details and examine specific issues likely to arise in the course of implementing an Enterprise Services Architecture. We start in this section with the problem of breaking down the larger project into a set of smaller deliverables.

From a design perspective, taking the big think and crafting a series of "little-bang" implementations can be very difficult. The idea of Enterprise Services Architecture is that a lot of moving parts are working together in some sort of ecosystem. How can an ecosystem be gradually introduced? When choosing the first milestone for an Enterprise Services Architecture implementation, concerns of building credibility and making a difference early should be part of the equation.

The first scenario we discussed provides some suggestions. For example, the right approach might be first to implement a portal layer, add adapters for enterprise applications to access more data and application functionality, and then add components for particular composite applications. It might also make sense to work one application at a time or one division at a time.

The prudent architect tries to choose a project that will have a significant impact but not be high risk. At the beginning of an Enterprise Services Architecture implementation, new skills are being learned, and such learning is not made easier by the glare of too much attention.

The first projects should be done in the background without massive deadline pressure to allow time for learning. A stage in the Rational Unified Process called "BLANK" scopes out the key architectural features of a large project. The fundamental issues that will govern the entire architecture are worked out. Remember that the vision of an Enterprise Services Architecture is generally so large that it can't be perfect in every way and will need to be adjusted. In the early projects, core components that bring up these fundamental issues should be developed to test the assumptions embedded in the architecture. The idea is to work on the plumbing and get that straight without having to debug in public.

Skill building is another important goal of early projects. If new technologies are being used or new relationships with integrators or new operational procedures are being adopted, time must be allotted for learning, misunderstandings, mistakes, and corrections. By the time the projects become highly visible, all of the skill building should have taken place.

As we mentioned at the end of the last chapter, implementing Enterprise Services Architecture requires a whole different set of operational skills. Operational preparation must come right from the start of the project because a set of components will be putting a new sort of demand on the operations team and they will need time to prepare. Change control is the same way. As a component architecture becomes more complex, it is harder to determine the impact of specific changes. Documenting the relationships between components is a skill that must be developed.

Going slow in the first few projects is often difficult after the initial internal sales process in which the value of the project was trumpeted to get approval. In fact, many IT projects are doomed from the beginning on this basis. The expectations set could never be met. Enterprise Services Architecture projects will be no different given the propensity of technologists to make exaggerated claims about the business value of technology.

Getting things right in the early stages of an Enterprise Services Architecture implementation is not just a politically prudent thing to do. Even though abstractions hide complexity and allow change underneath them, they themselves can become difficult to change as more systems rely on them. Remember the time example in the first chapter. It is a simple abstraction that is quirky given our decimal-oriented world, but it is so ingrained in our culture that it is unchangeable. The abstractions at the core of a component-based system are the same way. If they become popular, they are not easy to change. It is worth spending the time up front to make sure that they are as good as they can be.

Implementation Problems

After an Enterprise Services Architecture implementation project has been carved into stages and development is underway, a variety of problems will arise. Some of these are the familiar problems of software development in large projects. Others will be new problems unique to Enterprise Services Architecture. Here we provide a brief discussion of some of the most significant difficulties that are most likely to occur.

Network Speed and Capacity

Enterprise Services Architecture can put tremendous stress on the network. The connections that were taking place within the monolithic application are now taking place across the network. A slow network means a slow application. The increase in traffic could consume the capacity of the network and make it slow for everyone.

Application Consistency

APIs reach inside an application and provide access to data and functionality. One must be careful when poking around the internal organs of any software. Certain API calls are simple and well-behaved. Others are complex and difficult to understand. The consequences of a series of API calls may be difficult or impossible to predict even by the vendor of an application. Implementing Enterprise Services Architecture will bring these difficulties into play. Developers may become frustrated that an API call that should innocently provide data or a service may have damaging side effects. The fact that in many cases there is no process other than experimentation to find such side effects adds to the potential frustration and increases the need for thorough testing.

API Limitations

APIs were created for many different reasons, generally to allow an application to be integrated with other applications. In most cases, only a fraction of the functionality of an enterprise application is available as an API. A simple function that may be available in lots of different ways from the user interface may not be available as an API call.

Performance

Enterprise applications are generally constructed to provide excellent performance through the user interface and through API calls tuned for high performance. While building components in an Enterprise Services Architecture implementation, APIs may come under an unanticipated load and perform poorly. Fixing such problems may be difficult as the remedy requires changing the internal workings of an enterprise application or putting some buffering mechanism in place.

Too Much Translation

In many situations, components will be built from services that are provided by applications from different vendors. In such a situation, the data from one or both of the services must be transformed to a standard format. Data fields that are time-zone dependent or reflect different currencies, metrics, or encodings may have to be translated. One problem is maintaining the translations. The other is the impact that translating may have on performance. The sheer volume of translation needed to reconcile semantic differences may become a large performance bottleneck.

Change Management for Business Processes

Flexible processes at a technical level are only part of the requirement for a nimble enterprise. The people using the system must also be able to understand when a process changes and react differently. If a system is built to accommodate frequent process changes, users should be informed when processes are changed. Sometimes such information can be built into the user interface. Other times, processes outside the system must change and the changes must be communicated.

Operational Risk of Flexibility

In some cases, business staff will be able to configure processes and other application behavior. Care must be taken to make sure that the sorts of changes that can be implemented do not have disastrous effects. Either by training or by a user interface that ensures safety, business users must be prevented from changing the behavior of an application in harmful ways.

Operational Skills Gap

The operational skills needed to manage components are different in many ways from those needed to manage enterprise applications.

Every service needs a service level. Managing the proliferation of services can be quite difficult. The operations team should be brought in early to assess how they will handle the new world of components.

Operational Documentation

The relationships between objects in a monolithic application are not the concern of the operations department. They are inside the application, out of view. In an Enterprise Services Architecture, the relationships between components become an operational concern. When one component invokes the services of another, it needs network speed and reliability. The operations department must know about the dependencies between components to successfully manage downtime for system maintenance. Bringing one component down could crash the entire system.

Learning from Experience

The admission that no design is correct until it is implemented implies a responsibility to learn from experience and improve the design as problems come to light. The rookie hopes that nothing is going badly; the pro seeks out problems. In this section, we examine some questions and practices that may assist in the learning process as an Enterprise Services Architecture implementation proceeds.

Development Metrics

Development metrics can be a great help in boiling down the complexity of an Enterprise Services Architecture project for management and other external audiences. For example, when a project begins, it might be helpful to develop a set of metrics to gauge how much progress has been made in componentization. This might include indicators such as:

- Number of adapters built and deployed
- Number of components built and deployed

- Number of services available
- Number of new UI pages
- Number of composite applications

While none of these numbers can measure value, they can be helpful in demonstrating accomplishments during the early phases of a project when visible progress may be slow. At some point, when it is completely understood, a certain level of achievement can be used to declare victory (for example, celebrating when 100 components are available for reuse).

Operational Metrics

Operational metrics show how well the infrastructure is running and what parts are being used. They can indicate which components are critical to the operation of the system and the dependencies between components. Operational metrics for an Enterprise Services Architecture implementation might include:

- Services ranked by number of times invoked
- Services ranked by response time
- Components ranked by number of services invoked
- Components ranked by total CPU time consumed
- Network usage for intercomponent service calls
- Variance from minimum service levels

Metrics such as these reveal the critical path and the important relationships between components that can be used to optimize the infrastructure.

Component Size

At the beginning of an Enterprise Services Architecture implementation, the size of components tends not to be an issue. They are as big or as small as they need to be to do simple jobs like presenting the data from an application or coordinating a set of services. But as the number of components grows, the design problem becomes more complex and the issue of how much functionality to put in an individual component becomes quite difficult to resolve.

In one sense, it is impossible to know if you are getting it right until some unanticipated demand is made by new development. Ideally, when new demands are made on the system, many of the current components are relevant and only isolated changes are required.

This is an ancient design problem and we are not going to resolve it in this book. Here are some guidelines that indicate a problem with component size. Components may be too big if large chunks of the functionality are never used to satisfy most requests. If a component constantly requires changes when other components change, it could be too large as well. If no complexity is hidden, the component could be too small. If the number of dependencies between components is far larger than the number of components, the components may be too small.

If any of these problems arise, it generally requires a change in the design. In the next section, we describe how important decisions can be made in the context of a system of architectural governance, which is basically a long-term decision-making process about architecture.

Organizational Support for Enterprise Services Architecture

As we discuss in Chapter 9, Enterprise Services Architecture puts pressure on the traditional structure of a company. But for Enterprise Services Architecture to work in practice and allow for midcourse corrections, some specific organizational features are required.

For example, it is not uncommon for companies to have architectural councils that make pronouncements about "where we are going." The directives from such councils frequently come in the form of slender presentations with vague architectural diagrams and approved lists of vendors and system integrators. Sometimes, a consultant is brought in to create a detailed vision that quickly becomes outdated.

Active Design Team

Enterprise Services Architecture takes an incremental approach to implementation, along with adjustments of the vision based on experience. This strategy requires an active design team that stays current in its understanding of the detailed vision for the future and the current state of the implementation. Unlike an automobile where the design is completed and set in stone for the most part, in an Enterprise Services Architecture process, the design evolves as the implementation proceeds. The ability to move forward in an orderly manner requires an active design team.

This is much more easily said than done. Such an activity requires that careful long-term planning intrude on the crush of daily activities. It also requires a team that can take the time to understand the architecture, keep it in their brains, and envision how it should change based on the latest evidence. Keeping such a team active and in place is a tall order.

Efficient Decision Making

One of the reasons that most architectural councils are not terribly effective is that trade-offs are difficult. In the lean manufacturing model, one of the main jobs of the team leader is to force such trade-offs early in the process. Making such decisions is difficult, especially if some part of the organization loses out.

There is no easy solution to this problem. Tensions between power and competence must be resolved. The people who want to be on such a council to make decisions frequently do not have the time to keep a fresh vision of the architecture in their minds. The people who do (architects and engineers) sometimes are not fully aware of the business situation. A huge communications gap can develop between those with the detailed vision and those with the power. It is hard to recommend a general solution to this problem, but one way to resolve it is to include a nontechnical senior executive on the council who will be required to take the time to understand all of the issues and bring business perspective to the decision-making.

Political Challenges

In the face of corporate politics, Enterprise Services Architecture pretty much loses its distinctive character. Enterprise Services Architecture projects are subject to political forces like everything else in a company. Political barriers retard change at any organization. While there is no general cure for resistance to change, some ways to organize implementations make things easier.

Information helps to navigate the political minefield. The metrics mentioned earlier can help prove the value of Enterprise Services Architecture and show progress in a simplified manner.

Enterprise Services Architecture is not highly disruptive, which can also help. Enterprise Services Architecture is mostly about adding a layer that is orthogonal to existing technology rather than taking things away. New functionality shows up after the initial Enterprise Services Architecture technology is in place, and, if done right, this should make everyone happy. Only in the middle or later stages of an Enterprise Services Architecture implementation are some systems retired, which may ruffle some feathers.

The real political battles about Enterprise Services Architecture will probably take place as cross-functional automation and increased collaboration of composite applications call into question the traditional functional and geographic organization of most corporations. We will discuss this further in Chapter 9.

In the final analysis, an Enterprise Services Architecture implementation is a sustained research, design, and implementation project that should gradually create a more nimble enterprise. In the next chapter, we will examine the reaction of vendors of all sorts to the changes Enterprise Services Architecture will bring.

8

The Enterprise Value Chain

Enterprise Services Architecture is the latest extension of the modular approach to managing complexity. At first, all programs were monoliths. People coded what they needed. Then object-oriented programming was invented to manage the complexity of the monolith. Functionality was grouped together in objects that communicated through methods. Intraobject interaction was maximized; interobject interaction was minimized. Programs were more complex but more manageable, more flexible, and more reusable.

From the notion of an object, larger components were constructed. Most large applications have some subdivision of functionality, modules or components in which many objects are collected. The number of enterprise applications expanded and here we ran into trouble. The applications had components in them but these components were not easily reusable.

The next leap forward will take place as companies address Enterprise Services Architecture in their own business contexts. We will look at the value chain not from the perspective of a supply chain for a particular business, but by examining the tools that will be used to automate and streamline operations. We will examine how Enterprise Services Architecture will transform technology vendors and then discuss how the effects will ripple outward through the IT department and the corporation. In the next chapter we will discuss what will happen as the effect of Enterprise Services Architecture changes the marketplace, the economy, government, and society at large.

In our analysis, the growth of Enterprise Services Architecture has two stages. The first is the hybrid phase, in which components will be created on top of enterprise applications to provide the flexibility and agility to meet the demands of increasing competition.

We call this period the hybrid phase because the systems created will have features of the old monolithic enterprise applications and also of the newer world of components and services. The main job of the Enterprise Services Architecture platform is to serve the needs of the hybrid phase, in which components are crafted out of systems as described in preceding chapters. During this period, vendors will improve the componentization of the applications and the technology environment of application servers and standards like web services will evolve into more mature forms that are friendlier to componentization.

Perhaps one could identify the creation of CORBA as the beginning of the hybrid phase and the arrival of web services signaling broad participation. Web services and related standards make a componentized world practical, and, using them, the IT world will march forward toward increasing componentization.

The second phase is the service grid, a fully evolved environment in which standardized components and services can be easily deployed. In this phase, all elements of the infrastructure provide mature support for components.

In the service grid phase, the Enterprise Services Architecture platform will become invisible, just as accessing the Internet has become transparent. Some of us remember manually asking our modems to dial strings like "ATDT 9,555-1212" and installing a TCP/IP stack from vendors like Chameleon. These functions are vital but they have been standardized and commoditized. As a result, more people than ever use the Internet.

In the service grid era, the functions of the Enterprise Services Architecture platform will become widespread. Your phone will have web services interfaces and will be able to run downloaded components, perhaps the same ones that are running on the server. New sorts of pressures, demands, and skills will be required for everyone in the corporate world.

With the plumbing commoditized and reduced to invisibility, what will business and technology executives be thinking about? Process is the answer. The service grid will dramatically affect the effort that companies expend on understanding their processes, which ones they want to do well and which ones they want to outsource. Joshua Greenbaum, an analyst with Enterprise Applications Consulting, says, "Enterprise Services Architectures can only work if companies first understand and manage the processes that these architectures are designed to improve or rationalize."

Technology Vendors

Technology vendors have the most to gain and the most to lose from Enterprise Services Architecture. In this discussion, we mean technology vendors in the largest sense, including platform vendors that sell operating systems, databases, and application servers; application suite vendors that sell CRM, ERP, and other enterprise applications; independent software vendors (ISVs) that sell one enterprise application; and systems integrators who knit everything together.

As the IT industry proceeds from the hybrid phase into the service grid, extreme stress will be put on all of these companies. The challenges of addressing Enterprise Services Architecture will call into question their core competency, their ability to change, and the quality of their products.

In this section, we will examine how Enterprise Services Architecture and the forces toward components and services will cause vendors to reengineer their products and service offerings. We will look at how the vendors will fight it out to stake a claim on the new sort of applications that will be made possible, and we will look at what role each sort of vendor will play in the fully realized service grid.

Reengineering Monoliths into Components and Services

The first part of the hybrid phase is currently underway. Platform vendors are adding support for web services and related standards to application services. Application suite vendors and ISVs are exposing their applications as services. Systems integrators are learning to design architectures and applications based on components and services.

For the platform vendors, this is a familiar process. In the mid-1990s, they all had to learn to speak Java. Now they must learn to speak web services. They hope to do a better job of creating a development and integration environment than anyone else and thereby spread the adoption of their platform.

The same is true for system integrators. For them, Enterprise Services Architecture is another new trend to be understood and exploited for new business. In the same way that business process reengineering generated a lot of business in the early 1990s, systems integrators will find a way to generate useful projects out of the current transformation.

The application suite vendors and ISVs will have the toughest time and perhaps the most to gain. In the hybrid phase, the bill will come due for any shortcuts in engineering practices. It is not reasonable to blame anyone who has developed software over the past 20 years for creating a monolith. It was the most efficient way to create value for an enterprise application. But it means that the objects that form the central core of most enterprise applications are so tightly connected that it will be impossible to extract them and transform them incrementally. Most enterprise applications will have to be substantially rewritten in order to become a collection of components and services. This reconstruction will expose any weaknesses in engineering processes.

The challenge of rewriting enterprise applications will kill many companies. To make this transition, application suite vendors and

ISVs need advanced skills in architecture, modeling, design, product management, coding, testing, and packaging. They must manage and synchronize the life cycle of not only products but of individual components as well. All of these skills are required now, of course, but the same organization that supports current products will somehow have to create whole new products, not just incremental versions. This tsunami of change will be hard to manage.

For the application suite vendors and ISVs who get this right, a world of opportunity awaits. Enterprise applications that are fully componentized are much more valuable to both the vendor and the customer. The vendor can more easily take the same core application and create many more focused products for vertical markets or specific functions. Customers and systems integrators can use the products to create composite applications or integrations based on the components. Vendors will benefit further if certain components in their applications become the standard way to define and implement an important business function.

Application suite vendors and ISVs will have the opportunity to expand their businesses as well. The application suite vendors may be able to create a new development platform while the ISVs could get more systems integration work. But of course, platform vendors and systems integrators will fight back. We will examine this battle in the next section.

Vendor Conflicts

In the first book in this series, *Packaged Composite Applications*, we examined how the Enterprise Services Architecture platform will develop and how each type of vendor will probably react. Packaged Component Applications (PCAs) are products built on top of an Enterprise Services Architecture platform. We separated the components and services of the Enterprise Services Architecture platform and PCAs into three layers as show in Figure 8-1.

We argued that systems integrators and ISVs will fight it out at the PCA layer for the prize of creating the best vertically focused solu-

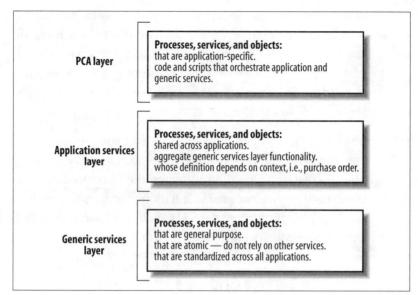

Figure 8-1. Definition of Enterprise Services Architecture layers

tions. Application suite vendors will also offer PCAs and will dominate the application services layer. Platform vendors will dominate the generic services layer.

The largest battle will be between the platform vendors and the application suite vendors to create the dominant Enterprise Services Architecture platform. The platform vendors' strength in the generic services layer and development environments will be pitted against the business-oriented components from the enterprise applications and application services of the suite vendors. Both companies bring platform component systems like content management to the table.

The battleground for the Enterprise Services Architecture platform is the hearts and minds of the architects of the IT departments. Application suite vendors are trying to leverage their installed base in order to create the most successful Enterprise Services Architecture platform. SAP, PeopleSoft, and Siebel all have products in this category. Platform vendors like IBM, Microsoft, and Sun are pushing their development platforms as the way to create a service-oriented architecture based on web services.

While most companies have accepted a heterogeneous world with products from many different vendors, it is unlikely that they will feel compelled to support many different Enterprise Services Architecture platforms. They will probably choose one, and the application suite vendors and the platform vendors will go to great lengths to make sure theirs gets chosen.

It is likely that a small number of companies will win and the others will line up in support of the victorious Enterprise Services Architecture platform, creating a situation in which the Enterprise Services Architecture platform becomes the foundation for enterprise applications, not simply an application server, which will have a profound effect on the architecture of enterprise applications.

Vendors in the Service Grid

When the hybrid phase is over and the Enterprise Services Architecture platform becomes a boring piece of the infrastructure, when adapters are no longer necessary because enterprise applications come as collections of components and services, when composite applications are easy to create and process models are the center of the IT infrastructure, in other words, when we have a fully implemented service grid, what will vendors be up to?

The world will certainly look different, and we examine the effect on the economy and marketplace in general in Chapter 9. The number of visible components and services will rise dramatically, creating operational and change management challenges that we will discuss in the next section. In this world vendors will likely fall into the following categories:

Platform providers

These are companies that sell the plumbing on which the service grid operates. It may be that one or two companies make a killing or at least a good living at this layer, or it could be that some new open-source garage band comes up with the next Linux or Apache that makes the service grid a commodity that customers get for free. The exciting new frontier for platform vendors will be in creating new model-driven ways of assembling and creating software that can be universally deployed. The platform vendors and application suite vendors of the hybrid phase fall into this category.

Orchestrators

These are companies that assemble applications and solutions. These companies, similar to auto manufacturers, will provide some components and services and use those from other companies to create applications. The applications will be able to be far more vertical than they are now because component architecture and the service grid will make supporting many different versions of a product far cheaper. Application suite vendors will sell products and systems integrators will provide custom orchestration.

Component and service providers

These are companies that sell components and services for use by orchestrators. This category is similar to the tier 1 and tier 2 suppliers in the auto industry. The service grid will allow much more specialization than is now possible. A small development team that creates the best component for name matching or some other function will have a much better chance of selling an application to a much larger market. ISVs will populate this category but it is likely that platform providers and orchestrators will also sell components and services to others.

Of course, all these vendors will push their products with the vendor's commercial interests in mind. We will now look at how companies that consume this technology will make sense of this new world starting with the IT department and then moving to the corporation at large.

Information Technology Organization

The impact of Enterprise Services Architecture will be felt first in the IT department. The marketing battle has already begun and service-

oriented products are showing up for general release. IT departments must now face the question of when and how to take action.
In Chapter 3, we examined pro and con arguments and in Chapters
6 and 7, we suggested how Enterprise Services Architecture could be
implemented most effectively. We now look at how the IT department will change in the hybrid phase and in the service grid phase.

Architecture, Design, and Process

As the barriers to change in the IT infrastructure drop, business and
technology executives will increasingly ask the question: Why did
we buy all this stuff in the first place?

The ultimate answer is to make more money. The mechanism is generally through using technology to increase efficiency or make better
products. The advent of Enterprise Services Architecture will greatly
expand the range of affordable next steps for the IT department.
Integration costs should drop. Assembling new applications should
be much easier. The potential to-do list will grow dramatically.

In this environment, deciding what to do next becomes a design
problem. How will every activity of the IT department fit into the
larger picture? Architecture becomes a crucial issue because, as we
pointed out in Chapter 6, the best IT departments will anticipate the
need for flexibility and prepare the infrastructure in advance. Even
with all of the flexibility of Enterprise Services Architecture, certain
architectural decisions will be hard to change. That is the essence of
good architecture: making the right decisions in areas that will have
an impact for a long time.

In modern day IT, architecture is a once a month activity, if that. As
we move through the hybrid phase toward the service grid, architecture will become a daily concern. Gathering evidence of how the
infrastructure ought to evolve will not happen once a year but all the
time, because it will be much easier to make adjustments. Wise IT
professionals will try to acquire and develop architecture and design
skills for their departments.

The focus of the design and architecture will be business processes. To succeed in extending automation of processes, the IT department will have to focus far more on understanding business operations than is currently the case. Business executives understand what they need to do to make money. IT professionals should provide the technical imagination so that process automation can be extended and improved in a series of practical steps that is consistent with a company's design and architectural strategy.

IT Operations in a World of Components

The rise of the Enterprise Services Architecture platform will have a dramatic effect on IT operations. Operations will become much more complex as connections between components multiply. In the monolithic world, each of the enterprise applications must be kept running fast enough and the connections between them must be monitored. In an Enterprise Services Architecture platform, each enterprise application is exploded into a number of components and the complexity of the operational environment rises dramatically. A handful of enterprise applications are replaced by a much larger number of components and services, each with its own service level. A small number of integrations between applications becomes a large number of connections between components. The rise in interdependency will lead to large challenges for performance tuning.

This daunting task will be made simpler in a few ways. A critical path of components and connections will probably be quickly identified for each enterprise application and this will become the focus of the most intense monitoring. The components are likely to come with fault tolerance, load balancing, and monitoring features to make the operational task easier. But, at the end of the day, an increase in operational complexity is the price of flexibility.

Another operational challenge is the increasing difficulty of change control in a world of many components. Keeping track of all this means that change control will be much more sophisticated and disciplined than it is currently. First, there is the basic documentation of all of the components in the architecture, where they are running, and how they are all connected. Next is understanding the impact of a change. A small change in the current operational environment can have dramatic effects. In an Enterprise Services Architecture with a larger number of connections between components, the effect of a small mistake could potentially be amplified to an even greater extent, which is likely to make VPs of operations even more paranoid than they already are.

The IT Department and the Service Grid

In a service grid, the operational difficulties of the hybrid era should have been solved to some extent. Components will probably implement standard frameworks for security, operational monitoring, and other functions that will make for a more stable environment. A more complex world will have to be managed, but there will be tools to help.

The core decision that the IT department must make about every component in the service grid era is, "Should we build, buy, or outsource?" Outsourcing will become more important because the plumbing of the service grid will make it cheaper and easier.

Enterprise Services Architecture will also lead to changes in the structure and skillsets of IT organizations. Internal development and operations teams may be split into different categories. Orchestration teams may glue things together into composite applications and component-based integrations. Service provider teams may focus on clusters of related components.

Even with a large degree of flexibility and many levels it will still be possible to create monoliths out of components. IT departments will be on the lookout to make sure that each incremental step maintains the evolvability of the architecture so that new processes and business relationships can be automated as fast as possible.

Enterprise Identity

At first, Enterprise Services Architecture will streamline the current way that a company does business. With the right architecture and design, components and services offered by an Enterprise Services Architecture platform will allow the IT department to be more responsive and say yes more often. Executives will find that IT is less of a bottleneck and that it offers them more choices.

Once the decks are cleared of the basic improvements that have been long delayed, the possibilities offered by Enterprise Services Architecture will start a conversation within most companies about central questions of corporate identity. In a situation hamstrung by limitations, the decision is generally which of several incremental improvements should be pursued. In other words, strategy and tactics are to some extent fixed. If it is possible to move in any direction, the question of which direction to take becomes more urgent. This is the business analog to the way design becomes more of a problem for IT architects because Enterprise Services Architecture offers more choices.

These changes will lead to an increased emphasis on process. Most organizations consciously manage and document processes in various ways. The understanding and automation of processes are generally bound by the capabilities of the current enterprise applications and hierarchical organizational structures. Enterprise Services Architecture breaks down these barriers and allows processes to be automated across functional and organizational boundaries, as well as between enterprises. This flexibility calls forth the question of what the right processes are and how they should be automated. Companies with an evolved understanding of their processes will be able to automate them more quickly and effectively.

As processes become the dominant structure in an organization, hierarchical forms of command and control start to creak. Individuals become identified more strongly with the potentially cross-functional and cross-divisional process teams in which they participate rather than with the functional, divisional, or geographic organization to which they are assigned. If an individual adds value primarily by helping a process that crosses these boundaries, performance metrics and incentives that do not reflect this reality will be misaligned or capricious. The right process-centric structure will vary widely from company to company.

Finally, we zero in on the most important question that Enterprise Services Architecture will lead companies to ask themselves: What is our core competency? In other words, how do we add value? What is it that we do for a living?

With the increasing choice in outsourcing various functions and the reduced cost and difficulty of integrating with partners, companies will have more scope to decide on which services and functions they choose to compete. Will the company be an orchestrator of a value chain or a participant in one or many by offering a service? A company must have a better grasp of its sustainable advantages in a world in which everyone is more nimble and flexible. The arrival of the service grid really doesn't change these questions or any of the other issues that Enterprise Services Architecture foists on companies, it just makes the need to address them more acute.

In the next chapter, we talk with Geoffrey Moore about the effect that widespread focus on core competency will have on the marketplace and the economy at large.

9

Enterprise Services
Architecture and Society

Just as Alan Greenspan acknowledged the positive effect of the Internet and information technology in explaining the length of the most recent period of sustained economic growth, someday the Chairman of the Federal Reserve will report to Congress or some other august group about the economic effects of Enterprise Services Architecture.

The chairman will look back on the current times from 5 or 10 years in the future and report how this period was the beginning of a profound change in how the economy was organized, driven by the lowering of transaction costs that service-oriented architecture brought about. The chairman's comments will surely recognize that companies in 2003 were under pressure from price deflation that created a relentless appetite for efficiency. Globalization resulted in cost reductions in the supply chain because of expanded opportunities for outsourcing and offshoring in a variety of countries.

But what sort of economy will emerge from this cauldron of forces? How will it affect relationships between consumers and companies? We turned to Geoffrey Moore, a consultant and venture capitalist, for an informed prediction.

Moore is best known for his classic analysis published in *Crossing the Chasm* (HarperBusiness), in which he explained how different strategies should be used to sell to different segments along the technology adoption curve. Moore pointed out that the strategy that benefits early adopters generally does poorly for the early majority, the next group of adopters. In his most recent book, *Living on the*

Fault Line (HarperBusiness), Moore examines how best to run a company to increase shareholder value using the concepts of core versus context activities that we will discuss later. Most recently he has been studying the effects of service-oriented architecture and how technology vendors and corporations should react.

Moore's analysis begins with a description of what is happening during the current hybrid period in which companies are doing their best to gain flexibility by crafting components and services from applications that were never meant to serve in such a capacity.

In Moore's view, the profound difference between the mainframe and client/server era and the current state of the art is that the emergence of the portal has promoted a user-centric view of the enterprise application. In previous generations, the database was king. The application and the user interface were tightly bound to the data being collected and managed. Data was something static to be retrieved, transformed, and stored again.

The user-centric view makes the needs of the individual and the role he or she is playing the primary focus. These needs are unlikely to map precisely to the data within one and only one enterprise application. Service-oriented architectures like Enterprise Services Architecture solve this problem by creating services that can bring information from a variety of applications into one user interface.

A conceptual transformation also takes place, from dealing with nouns and inert data, to verbs and services that actively perform some task and have the ability to provide abstraction.

Moore sees the components used to bring such applications to life as falling into two natural groups. One group of components will be focused on managing interaction with the user and collaboration. The other group will form a structure like a router or switch. Hubs representing customer, product, or employee data will manage the task of unifying information in distributed repositories.

In the hybrid period, with the Enterprise Services Architecture platform enabling applications from the era of nouns to provide value in a emerging world of verbs, there will be some growing pains.

"The growth of service-oriented architecture has to happen. The only question is how clunky it will be," says Moore. "Even if it is clunky at first and the performance is annoying, it can still add a lot of value."

Moore predicts that the first implementations of service-oriented architectures will take place inside the enterprise. Once problems of security and operational stability are worked out, trusted partners will be brought into the architecture. External relationships will be handled easily through simple interfaces. Moore predicts the most difficult relationships to automate and bring into a service-oriented architecture will be those between the close, trusted partners and the distant external relationships. He expects that five years from now, such relationships will still represent a challenge.

Moore thinks that several reactionary forces will retard the adoption of service-oriented architectures. The dearth of truly talented process-modeling and design skills, which have always been in short supply, will be even more of a problem. Companies with relationships that may be displaced, as well as employees who may lose their jobs in this new world, will also fight against change.

But Moore sees some tremendous benefits from the rise in service-oriented architecture that are closely related to his concept of core versus context activities. Core activities differentiate a company from all others in the marketplace and are the key to creating value. Context activities enable core activities to take place. In fast-changing industries, core activities become context after a while because the rest of the marketplace may learn how to perform a core activity. In *Living on the Fault Line*, Moore describes a diverse collection of forces that lead companies to expend far too much of their resources on context activities, which has the effect of diluting the return on invested capital.

One company's context may be another's core. The path to the maximum return on capital therefore is to focus a firm's resources on core activities and outsource the context activities to other companies who may offer such services as their core activity. At the limit of this structure, with all companies adopting this policy, no firm does any activity that is not core, and systemwide returns should rise.

Of course, this limit case is only theoretical and will never be reached in practice. But the forces driving companies in this direction are real, and Enterprise Services Architecture is a key enabler because it dramatically lowers the cost of outsourcing and expands the number of activities that could potentially be outsourced.

Moore predicts that for companies in industries where one company orchestrates a virtual supply chain, service-oriented architectures will be vital to success. These companies will have to be incredibly process-centric to succeed. They will have to deeply understand their processes in order to craft and manage the right outsourcing relationships.

For companies in industries that are focused on the command and control of the activities within one organization, service-oriented architectures will help improve efficiency across the board in both core and context activities. A focus on flexible process automation based on services will be most appropriate in core activities.

Moore sees the ultimate economic effect of service-oriented architecture as a reduction in the annoyances of everyday life. He predicts that efficiencies will primarily apply to administrative and compliance activities such as paying taxes, filing expense reports, paying traffic tickets, setting up health insurance, or getting a driver's license. With the proper set of services, Moore imagines that the kind of agents that were once thought of as searching the Internet to find the best price on a watch are actually saving you time by handling tedious administrative tasks.

"You free up human capital waiting on line in the DMV and the people serving them," Moore says. "What would happen to your life if you never had to be in voice mail jail again? The return for the consumer is more free time."

Moore sees the ultimate impact of service-oriented architecture as an incremental improvement toward a more efficient society. For some industries it will be a revolution, but for most the change will be the welcome arrival of technology that has tangible benefit.

Building on Moore's vision, it is possible to envision some interesting battles in the future. David Mitchell Smith, VP and Gartner Fellow at Gartner Research, argues that if service-oriented architecture makes outsourcing effortless, it is easily possible to see a massive political backlash against the shifting of jobs and investment. Right now, an email sent to customer service at Amazon.com or an x-ray at a large hospital may actually be processed in another country. If service-oriented architecture dramatically accelerates such outsourcing, those losing out may seek to make such activities illegal and spark a trade war in services.

Privacy is another area that service-oriented architecture will bring to higher prominence. Outsourcing means that customer information and other sensitive data will be crossing many more corporate and perhaps international boundaries. Differences in regulations across governmental boundaries could be a barrier to adoption or the focus of concern from privacy advocates.

The most significant impact of service-oriented architectures like Enterprise Services Architecture will probably surprise us all. Perhaps at the center of these trends is a force that will compel both companies and individuals to more completely understand what we are good at and what we must focus on to succeed. We sincerely hope that our tour of Enterprise Services Architecture and all its implications proves helpful in that endeavor.

Afterword
Enterprise Services Architecture and the Adaptive Enterprise

If there were a single word to describe business—or even personal—life in the current world, it would be adaptive. We as individuals find ourselves challenged by change on a scale and frequency never before seen. Demands in the workplace to achieve the impossible, accept the inevitable, and adapt to the changes demanded of us never seem to cease. Yet these demands are no more or less than the personalization of the situation facing our employers as the enterprises for whom we work struggle to meet, accommodate, and rise above the demands of the external marketplaces.

However, some enterprises still seem to prosper and thrive on these conditions. Constant change seems to suit them—indeed, it seems to be part of their business model. They are *adaptive enterprises* where change is built into the very genes of their strategy. Acceptance of and perhaps even a desire for change runs throughout their culture. For such enterprises, change that satisfies customers is a key part of their competitive success.

This flies in the face of conventional business wisdom under which specialization leads to optimization, which makes change expensive. IT in particular is regularly cited by executive-level management as a barrier to change. In short, to be an adaptive enterprise means having adaptive IT. In practice, it is arguably the other way around: if an enterprise has adaptive IT, it can change and even use the speed with which it can change as a competitive weapon, thus becoming an adaptive enterprise.

The key to achieving such adaptability is the increased abstraction, componentization, and loose coupling described in this book. There are many paths to adaptability, but in my experience the assumptions of Enterprise Services Architecture embody the guidelines that can give a company the best chance for success.

This complicated and complex subject was recognized and studied by Cap Gemini Ernst & Young in the mid-1990s. In a book titled *Blur: The Speed of Change in the Connected Economy* (Perseus), Chris Meyer of the Cap Gemini Ernst & Young Center for Business Innovation argued that three forces were affecting business and would affect all enterprises: speed, intangibles, and connectivity. According to Meyers, "As these three forces converge, every dimension of business behavior is being challenged to the core. If you think that business can be sustained by the old rules of mass production, segment pricing, and stable organizations, you'll need to think again. Welcome to the new economy—a world where the rate of change is so fast it is only a blur, where the clear lines distinguishing buyer from seller, product from service, employee from entrepreneur are disappearing. To profit from these revolutionary patterns of business you need a dynamic guide to the new economy."

This work started within Cap Gemini Ernst & Young on managing change in real enterprises. Indeed exactly as the book foretold, it also led to strong cooperation and interaction with partners such as SAP to make the reality achievable with solid, well-built IT solutions.

In 1999, a Cap Gemini Ernst & Young technology white paper called "The Business Models for Connected Enterprises and the Consequences for Technical Architecture" argued that IT would need to change from the application-centric client/server model into a process-centric architecture permitting rapid combination and recombination of users and applications through the introduction of a flexible process layer.

Enterprise Services Architecture provides exactly this sort of flexibility. Loosely coupled components and services can be rapidly recombined to create composite applications. User interface abstraction brings these applications to new groups of users with a targeted user interface. Process abstraction, the highest level of Enterprise Services Architecture compliance, allows optimization of business processes.

The arguments for why this is needed have already been given in earlier chapters, so this afterword focuses on business issues. Part of this analysis addresses how the CIO and IT departments will need to change their thinking, approach, and management metrics to achieve adaptive IT to support the adaptive enterprise.

What then is the case for the adaptive enterprise? The study of successful adaptive enterprises can be of particular value in identifying the way that being adaptive pays off and how to achieve this state.

Some industries have been truly transformed already by innovators using technology-induced business improvement. Consider the impact of eBay on the automotive market: it has become the largest seller of used cars in North America. Expedia is now the world's largest travel agent. Dell reformed the expectations of the PC market. All of these companies, none of which existed in any significant manner prior to the Internet, are now world leaders, and all demonstrate that the Internet really changed process through interaction, not merely content as was predicted. The message is that adaptive automation of process is the lever that brings tangible business success.

It's not only the Internet babies that have proved this: existing businesses of all sizes and sorts have learned how to apply adaptive processes to some part of their business or brand. The challenge lies in proving it, and applying it, in a manner that the boardroom can accept, given its duty of caring for shareholders, employees, and customers. Figure A-1 helps to delineate the business value of adaptive processes in the current business climate.

The old world lies in the two left-hand boxes, where the rate of change was low and, more importantly, was likely to be under the control of the enterprise itself. In the old world, the boundary around the enterprise and its way of functioning was high, the incidence of global competition was low, and the very speed by which change could occur was limited due to lack of communication

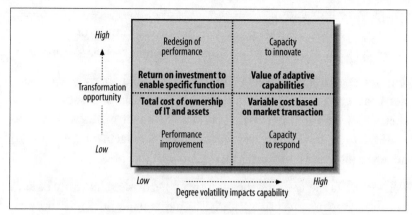

Figure A-1. Potential performance improvements versus volatility

media. Change could be managed internally with no visibility to the outside world. Internal processes were optimized and automated around departmental applications and eventually around ERP that spanned departmental boundaries and made a huge difference in internal productivity and other business benefits.

The new world lies in the right-hand boxes where volatility is high (and therefore change is constant) and adaptive behavior that is visible to the marketplace is the key to success. Two important skills are needed. The first is responding to changes in external conditions, clearly necessary for basic survival. The second and perhaps more important is changing how the market works to pressure competitors into responding. This is where real success and profitability lies. It requires mastery of two different domains that are seldom found together—business and technology—and the ability to have integrated comprehension. This is the key observation of the long journey made by Cap Gemini Ernst & Young chronicled at the beginning of the chapter.

Consider the way that IT investment and operational budgets are justified in Figure A-2.

The names of departments and functions in Figure A-2 are purely examples; any department, function, application, or process could be used. The vertical axis refers to the degree of business importance while the horizontal axis indicates the degree of volatility.

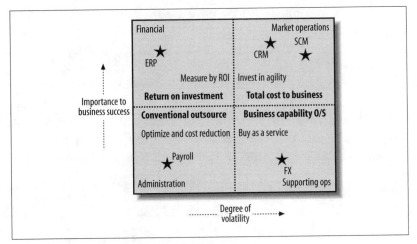

Figure A-2. Business value versus volatility

Again the old world lies to the left; if it is really important to the enterprise, and stable, it can be built to be good enough, which means it is context not core, in the sense Geoffrey Moore pointed out in the last chapter. In this well-understood environment, ROI is the long accepted method of measuring the need to act and the benefit of action. Stable activities related to context are located in the lower-left quadrant. The cost of supplying the minimum required functionality becomes the issue leading to a classic build versus buy outsourcing analysis.

Many CFOs and senior managers are not convinced that ROI is really being achieved with many projects today. In some cases, ROI models are a farce, cobbled together to support must-do projects where the intuitive operational logic is obvious, but the financial case is not. These sorts of projects usually belong in the upper-right quadrant. Their importance is high, and they are probably needed to enable a rapid response to external market-driven activity. They are rarely stable enough to apply a traditional ROI analysis. Email is a classic example: there is no known example of ROI being successfully applied to implementing email. On the other hand, though there are undoubtedly moments when we would all wish email was not there, its continued role in supporting adaptive behavior in and between enterprises is unquestionable. Without it, most enterprises simply could not function in an acceptable manner in the face of today's needs.

Clearly, a different approach is called for. For want of a better name, we will call it "cost to business," though "value to business" might be an alternative title with more appeal. The implications of this approach are many and profound, but the basic technique is clear and simple to explain. The business case for value is made around the opportunity cost, both in terms of what it enables, and in terms of the cost of opportunity lost without the implementation. The IT case is made around the initial setup cost in addition to the cost of ongoing operations that enable incremental improvement and change. This second point is vital. Building a system without ensuring evolvability dooms it to failure. This is the whole key to the Cap Gemini Ernst & Young adaptive IT model that supports the move to delivering solutions based on the mantra of "build to perform, architect to change." As any CIO will attest, the majority of the budget goes to maintenance, not to new initiatives. Build in evolvability and the payoff dividend is immense.

What of the lower-right quadrant? Here it is of less importance to the business, but classic outsourcing arrangements that assume stability won't work. Business Process Outsourcing, or BPO, could be the answer, if it can handle the volatility. But frequently it can't because BPO usually assumes stability. Business Capability Outsourcing, or BCO, may work better because it emphasizes a relationship in which the partner has a collection of capabilities that can support regular change and employs a business model that accommodates flexibility in terms of the cost of changes.

These important issues underpin an analysis of what success means, without which Enterprise Services Architecture cannot be adequately applied. In Figure A-3, we look at the factors that are key to business success versus volatility.

Here two new technology terms enter our two-by-two matrix: mobility and grids. The diagram demonstrates how issues related to creating adaptive IT are also critical preparations for the future where

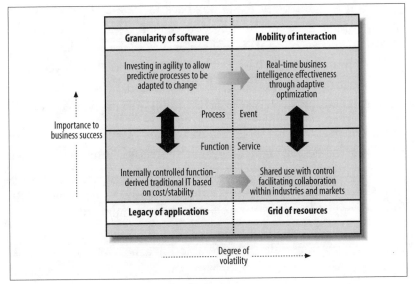

Figure A-3. Business success versus volatility

there is an increasingly externalized role for IT. Maybe first it is worth recalling the old business axiom that business is made up of only three fundamental activities:

1. Buy something

2. Add value

3. Sell it

Two of these activities are external and are the activities through which external pressure is applied to the corporation, leading to the need for internal adaptive behavior and capabilities. However, the internal reform that is needed will both lead to, and benefit from, the external reform of the market, or at least an industry ecosystem. *Mobility* correctly interpreted means the "Internet of things," covering everything from sensors to handheld devices and much more, connecting as—and when—needed to interact. *Grid* on the other hand represents the resources underlying this model to support the interaction. Today this means hardware, but just as Enterprise Resource Planning is becoming Network Resource Planning, this represents a future move to Dynamic Resource Planning.

This returns to the point made way back in 1998 by Chris Meyer in his book *Blur*: "Welcome to the new economy—a world where the rate of change is so fast it is only a blur, where the clear lines distinguishing buyer from seller, product from service, employee from entrepreneur are disappearing. To profit from these revolutionary patterns of business you need a dynamic guide to the new economy."

So in conclusion what does all this mean? Maybe the degree of change it implies is frightening, and the classic response to being frightened is to either freeze (do nothing) or flee (go and find some diversionary activity that looks promising but is not so challenging). Either would be a mistake; as in all things, timing is all. Starting early and small, rather than starting late and needing to immediately change on a large scale, is preferable for a host of good reasons. Enterprise Services Architecture is the sound way of achieving this: it is a well-constructed overall program, dealing with things that are perhaps of no concern on today's smaller project but will become of concern as this project expands and needs to interact with other projects. It is a great way to get short-term wins in a long-term game by building on past success with the existing systems. Nobody in business, or IT, is going to complain about that route. Justification methods for small projects piloting new abilities can be more relaxed to allow experimentation with the metrics by which business value is identified.

The road map to being an adaptive enterprise capable of finding success in this increasingly volatile world based on adaptive IT is to start right now to move through three stages that ensure risks are minimized and returns are maximized:

Adopt
> Pilot using the new approach and capabilities of Enterprise Services Architecture to build quick wins and gain confidence in how, where, and when to apply and justify.

Adapt

Extend the use and capabilities to increasingly embrace existing (and probably non-SAP) systems at incremental cost with exponential gains.

Transform

Innovate for true competitive advantage from the secure foundation that this approach has built.

—Andy Mulholland
Chief Technology Officer
Cap Gemini Ernst & Young
July 4, 2003

Index

We'd like to hear your suggestions for improving our indexes. Send email to *index@oreilly.com*.

199

About the Author

Dan Woods is CTO and Publisher of the Evolved Media Network, a consulting and publishing firm that provides services for technology communications. Dan has a background in technology and journalism. He has a BA in computer science from the University of Michigan. He was CTO of *TheStreet.com* and CapitalThinking, led development at Time Inc.'s Pathfinder, and created applications for *NandO.net*, one of the first newspaper web sites. Dan has an MS from Columbia University's Graduate School of Journalism. He covered banking for three years at *The Record of Hackensack*, was database editor for three years at the *Raleigh News & Observer*, and has written several books on technology topics, in addition to numerous white papers and magazine articles. He lives in New York City with his wife and two children. Dan can be reached at *dwoods@EvolvedMediaNetwork.com*.

Colophon

Our look is the result of reader comments, our own experimentation, and feedback from distribution channels. Distinctive covers complement our distinctive approach to technical topics, breathing personality and life into potentially dry subjects.

Darren Kelly was the production editor, Debra Cameron was the developmental editor, and Sada Preisch was the proofreader for *Enterprise Services Architecture*. Claire Cloutier provided quality control. Julie Hawks wrote the index.

Edie Freedman designed the cover of this book. The cover image is an original color engraving from the 19th century. Emma Colby produced the cover layout with QuarkXPress 4.1 using Myriad and Birka fonts.

David Futato and Edie Freedman designed the interior layout. This book was converted by Joe Wizda to FrameMaker 5.5.6 with a format conversion tool created by Erik Ray, Jason McIntosh, Neil Walls, and Mike Sierra that uses Perl and XML technologies. The text font is Linotype Birka; the heading font is Adobe Myriad Condensed; and the code font is LucasFont's TheSans Mono Condensed. The illustrations that appear in the book were produced by Robert Romano and Jessamyn Read using Macromedia FreeHand 9 and Adobe Photoshop 6.

About O'Reilly

O'Reilly & Associates is the premier information source for leading-edge computer technologies. The company's books, conferences, and web sites bring to light the knowledge of technology innovators. O'Reilly books, known for the animals on their covers, occupy a treasured place on the shelves of the developers building the next generation of software. O'Reilly conferences and summits bring alpha geeks and forward-thinking business leaders together to shape the revolutionary ideas that spark new industries. From the Internet to XML, open source, .NET, Java, and web services, O'Reilly puts technologies on the map.

For more information, see *www.oreilly.com*

O'REILLY®